Volume I
Publicatio
April 197,

Psychiatry and Sex Psychopath Legislation: The 30s to the 80s

Formulated by the
Committee on Psychiatry and Law

WITHDRAWN

Group for the Advancement of Psychiatry

This publication was produced for the Group for the Advancement of Psychiatry by the Mental Health Materials Center, Inc., New York

International Standard Book Number 0-87318-135-2

Library of Congress Catalog Card Number 77-72874

Printed in the United States of America

TABLE OF CONTENTS

This is the eighth in a series of publications comprising Volume IX. For a list of the other GAP publications on current topics of interest, see last page of book herein.

STATEMENT OF PURPOSE

THE GROUP FOR THE ADVANCEMENT OF PSYCHIATRY has a membership of approximately 300 psychiatrists, most of whom are organized in the form of a number of working committees. These committees direct their efforts toward the study of various aspects of psychiatry and the application of this knowledge to the fields of mental health and human relations.

Collaboration with specialists in other disciplines has been and is one of GAP's working principles. Since the formation of GAP in 1946 its members have worked closely with such other specialists as anthropologists, biologists, economists, statisticians, educators, lawyers, nurses, psychologists, sociologists, social workers, and experts in mass communication, philosophy, and semantics. GAP envisages a continuing program of work according to the following aims:

1. To collect and appraise significant data in the fields of psychiatry, mental health, and human relations
2. To reevaluate old concepts and to develop and test new ones
3. To apply the knowledge thus obtained for the promotion of mental health and good human relations

GAP is an independent group, and its reports represent the composite findings and opinions of its members only, guided by its many consultants.

PSYCHIATRY AND SEX PSYCHOPATH LEGISLATION: THE 30s TO THE 80s was formulated by the Committee on Psychiatry and Law, which acknowledges on page 837 the participation of a consultant in the preparation of this report. The members of this committee are listed below. The following pages list the various other committees, other membership categories as well as current officers of GAP.

COMMITTEE ON PSYCHIATRY AND LAW

Carl P. Malmquist, Minneapolis, MN, Chairman

Edward T. Auer, Philadelphia, PA
Elissa P. Benedek, Ann Arbor, MI
John Donnelly, Hartford, CT

James B. Funkhouser, Richmond, VA
Robert S. Garber, Belle Mead, NJ
Alicia Gavalya, Allston, MA
Donald J. Scherl, Boston, MA
Herzl R. Spiro, Milwaukee, WI
Jack A. Wolford, Pittsburgh, PA

COMMITTEE ON MENTAL RETARDATION
Thomas G. Webster, Washington, DC,
    Chairman
Howard V. Bair, Parsons, KS
Norman R. Bernstein, Boston, MA
Leo Madow, Philadelphia, PA
Carolyn B. Robinowitz, Bethesda, MD
George Tarjan, Los Angeles, CA
Warren T. Vaughan, Jr., Portola Valley, CA
Henry H. Work, Washington, DC

COMMITTEE ON PREVENTIVE PSYCHIATRY
E. James Lieberman, Washington, DC,
    Chairman
Charles M. Bryant, San Francisco, CA
Jules V. Coleman, New Haven, CT
Stephen Fleck, New Haven, CT
Frederick Gottlieb, Los Angeles, CA
Ruth W. Lidz, Woodbridge, CT
Richard G. Morrill, Roxbury, MA
Harris B. Peck, Bronx, NY
Marvin E. Perkins, White Plains, NY

COMMITTEE ON PSYCHIATRY AND COMMUNITY
Alexander S. Rogawski, Los Angeles, CA,
    Chairman
C. Knight Aldrich, Charlottesville, VA
Lee B. Macht, Cambridge, MA
Herbert C. Modlin, Topeka, KS
John C. Nemiah, Boston, MA
Anthony F. Panzetta, Philadelphia, PA
John J. Schwab, Louisville, KY
Charles B. Wilkinson, Kansas City, MO

COMMITTEE ON PSYCHIATRY AND POLITICS
Robert N. Butler, Washington, DC, Chairman
Paul Chodoff, Washington, DC
Jerome D. Frank, Baltimore, MD
Judd Marmor, Los Angeles, CA
Montague Ullman, Ardsley, NY

COMMITTEE ON PSYCHIATRY AND RELIGION
Albert J. Lubin, Woodside, CA, Chairman
Sidney S. Furst, Bronx, NY

Richard C. Lewis, New Haven, CT
Mortimer Ostow, Bronx, NY
Michael R. Zales, Greenwich, CT

COMMITTEE ON PSYCHIATRY IN INDUSTRY
Herbert L. Klemme, Stillwater, MN,
    Chairman
Barrie S. Greiff, Boston, MA
Duane Q. Hagen, St. Louis, MO
R. Edward Huffman, Asheville, NC
Alan A. McLean, New York, NY
David E. Morrison, Topeka, KS
Clarence J. Rowe, St. Paul, MN
John A. Turner, San Francisco, CA
John Wakefield, Saratoga, CA

COMMITTEE ON PSYCHOPATHOLOGY
Charles Shagass, Philadelphia, PA, Chairman
Aaron T. Beck, Wynnewood, PA
Wagner H. Bridger, Bronx, NY
Paul E. Huston, Iowa City, IA
Richard E. Renneker, Los Angeles, CA
A. John Rush, Oklahoma City, OK

COMMITTEE ON PUBLIC EDUCATION
Robert J. Campbell, New York, NY, Chairman
Mildred Mitchell Bateman, Charleston, WV
James A. Knight, College Station, TX
John P. Lambert, Katonah, NY
Norman L. Loux, Sellersville, PA
Mabel Ross, Chicago, IL
Julius Schreiber, Washington, DC
Robert H. Sharpley, Cambridge, MA
Miles F. Shore, Boston, MA
Robert A. Solow, Beverly Hills, CA
Kent A. Zimmerman, Berkeley, CA

COMMITTEE ON RESEARCH
Alfred H. Stanton, Wellesley Hills, MA,
    Chairman
Robert Cancro, New York, NY
Stanley H. Eldred, Belmont, MA
John G. Gunderson, Belmont, MA
Jerry M. Lewis, Dallas, TX
Morris A. Lipton, Chapel Hill, NC
John G. Looney, Dallas, TX
Ralph R. Notman, Brookline, MA
Charles P. O'Brien, Philadelphia, PA
John S. Strauss, Rochester, NY
Herbert Weiner, Bronx, NY

834

COMMITTEE ACKNOWLEDGMENT

The Committee would like to express its appreciation to its consultant, Norval Morris, who is Julius Kreeger Professor of Law and Criminology and dean of the Law School of the University of Chicago. His critique and searching questions were of much help in the middle phase of this study.

Carl P. Malmquist, M.D.

1

THE PROBLEM OF "SEX PSYCHOPATHS" AND SEX PSYCHOPATH STATUTES

Anyone who imposes his diverse or perverse sexual desires upon another in a coercive manner provokes powerful emotions in a community. This report is concerned with individuals whose potential to behave in such a manner incurs criminal sanctions. They have either violated the criminal law by their sexual conduct and are legally convicted of a sex offense, or they are perceived as having the potential to behave in a sexually dangerous manner and become sex criminals in the future. We see special sex offender legislation as an approach to sex psychopaths that has failed, and consequently we feel that these statutes should be repealed.

In 1950 GAP published its first and only report dealing with the problem of "psychiatrically deviated sex offenders."[1] A reappraisal of the original concepts in the light of the intervening decades is sorely needed, especially in view of the ferment that grows in the United States when any group is so singled out. Accordingly, this report is primarily addressed to mental health professionals who work as clinicians or administrators with these individuals, as well as attorneys, members of the judiciary, legislators, and interested lay persons.

The goals of the report are: (1) to describe historically how criminal sexual conduct was handled before special sex psychopath statutes were created in the 1930s; (2) to examine the types of statutes enacted specifically to deal with classes of individuals described by special terms, such as "sex offenders" or "sexual psychopaths"; (3) to explore the conceptual framework of the "sexual psychopath," as well as the confusion attendant upon the use of such categories; (4) to appraise the current status of the treatments that are being used with sex offenders. An examination of the problems attendant upon the use of technologies that have been available as treatments and that involve problems of informed consent is needed, and lastly, (5) to investigate the role of the psychiatrist as an evaluator of these individuals and as a clinician who participates in the legal system.

In retrospect, we view the sex psychopath statutes as social experiments that have failed and that lack redeeming social value. These experiments have been carried out by the joint participation of the psychiatric and legal professions with varying degrees of acquiescence by the general public. The reasons for our position advocating repeal are discussed in this report.

The need to clarify terminology

There is an immediate need for clarification of terms. *Sexual psychopathy* is not a psychiatric diagnosis. It is a term used with a variety of confusing meanings and applications but with no precise clinical meaning. Also, since sex psychopaths are defined in statutes, the term is therefore an established legal concept. Definitions of statutes of sex psychopaths which arose in the 1930s were taken from a confluence of sources. Legislative bodies drew on an amalgam of psychiatric and social concepts to encompass a heterogeneous group of individuals seen as dangerous with respect to control over their sexual behavior but not seen as legally insane. Their actual psychiatric status and diagnoses varied widely then and now. (For examples of definitions promulgated by legislative bodies see Chapter 4.) The pervasive theme in the enactment of such sex statutes was the belief that certain individuals would fail to control their sexual behavior or idiosyncrasies and that they could consequently be identified and segregated. In this sense, the grouping was analogous to that of individuals classified as possessing a certain propensity, such as drug addiction or alcoholism. They were to be dealt with even though they were not at present violating any law. Although women could be processed under these special sex statutes, the nature of the sexual behavior encompassed under sexual psychopathy involved few women other than as victims or accomplices.

It is important to keep in mind two confusing usages of the term "sexual psychopath." It is used one way when an individual is before a court and a decision must be made to exclude or include him within the legal definition of sexual psychopath. He need not necessarily have even committed a sex crime, depending on the state in question and its statutes. A second usage, based on a clinical or epidemiological notion, refers to those persons within a community who would meet a given definition if some type of case-finding were instituted. This latter meaning would cover persons not yet brought to the attention of a court, as well as a subset of individuals who have been brought into court for sexual behavior that has violated the law.

In contrast, a *sex offender* is a person who has been charged and found guilty of a particular sex crime. Some states have provided for special handling and disposition of these individuals. As such, the number and types of sex crimes that come under the special sentencing provisions vary from state to state. It is further confusing when some states have one statute to deal with sex psychopaths and a *separate* statute for sex offenders; other states have one or the other. Some have none but simply list certain sex crimes as part of the general criminal code. Straight conviction and sentencing was the prescribed procedure before special sex legislation was enacted.

Special statutes as alternatives

Sex psychopath statutes had their ideologic origins in the 1930s. They were viewed as alternatives to straight imprisonment for handling people who either had behaved sexually in a manner that got them into difficulties with the criminal law or who were seen as having the potential to do so. The "sex statutes" were meant to be harbingers of a future in which all criminals would be "treated" under similar provisions. The sex statutes in question, while categorized somewhat differently by various state legislatures, have customarily involved offenses such as rape, aggravated rape, indecent liberties, sodomy, certain sexual acts with minors, incest, or attempts to commit some of these acts. The exact wording varies somewhat from statute to statute, but all such laws focus upon sexual acts of a threatening or violent nature or on those involving legal minors. Less threatening acts of a sexually deviant or dysfunctional nature (e.g., homosexuality between consenting adults, exhibitionism, and voyeurism) are usually not included. Some behavior, such as bestiality, may or may not be included.

Although the history of the sex statutes emphasizes dual goals—community safety and treatments—their origin appears more closely tied to desires of legislators to protect their constituents. The preservation of community safety is encompassed within the police power of the state, while any treatment measures are carried out under the *parens patriae* duty of the state to rehabilitate its wayward citizens. Under one or both of these banners, diverse treatment measures have been carried out. These vary from medical treatment (as contrasted with social treatment), an alternative to sentencing, and psychological or physical means of altering behavior.

It has now been more than 30 years since the "experiment" was initiated to define sex psychopaths and create special sex statutes. Some states have already begun to repeal these outmoded laws. Our position is that the experiment was a form of well intentioned but misguided intervention. Its dual goals have often remained in conflict. After a given passage of time an experiment needs evaluation in terms of its demonstrable benefits and liabilities. If the assessment of the statute in terms of achieving certain goals, for whatever reasons, leads to the conclusion that an experiment has not been successful, it should be halted.

Another element is relevant: There is not only the problem of failure to attain the positive ends sought, but there is also the need to appraise the adverse aspects involving individuals or society which can develop when sought-after goals are not achieved. It may be that achieving certain goals requires subjecting a person to a treatment that can harm his physical or psychological integrity. Indeterminate institutionalization or the utilization of questionably experimental procedures are examples that need careful scrutiny and assessment. The balancing of individual rights against societal needs remains as a paramount problem. Similarly, too ardent a pursuit of goals may involve high social costs as well, such as loss of personal freedom for excessive periods of time or invasions of privacy that are not readily acceptable.

A significant number of legal and mental health professionals, as well as laymen, disagree with the specific opinions expressed in this report and especially with our recommendation that special sex psychopath statutes should be totally repealed. Many support continuation of the "experiment" as a price for community security. Some prefer to continue with these statutes as alternatives to the criminal justice route for punishment of the sex offender. Others recommend substantial modification of these statutes such as changing indeterminate commitment of the sexual psychopath to a determinate judicial commitment with periodic review. Still others prefer moving from involuntary treatment to voluntary treatment with informed consent or to involuntary treatment of the sexual psychopath on a monitored outpatient basis.

A brief historical survey will aid in the understanding of how we have arrived at our present dilemmas with respect to criminal sexual conduct. We can gain perspective by seeing how these same problems have remained throughout the centuries and by noting the different approaches tried in different historical and social settings. This is the background that ultimately gave rise to the special sex psychopath statutes as a proposed solution in the 1930s.

2

BACKGROUND HERITAGE

Individuals whose sexual behavior is contrary to the mores of a given community have usually been dealt with by courts designating them as "socially deviant." Definitions of what constitutes an actual sexual crime have varied, as have their accompanying dispositions. A historical analysis of the ways in which persons defined as sexual criminals were handled within the confines of the Anglo-American legal system is valuable from the perspective it gives to recent efforts to control such conduct. It should not come as a surprise that behavioral control, under diverse names, has been sought for centuries.

Under the system of English common law, ecclesiastical courts originally exercised a wide jurisdiction over all matters pertaining to morals and the family. These courts assumed jurisdiction with the hope of amelioration in contrast to the harsher penalties exacted under the general criminal juridication. Apart from offenses specifically punishable at common law, the church claimed residual jurisdiction over acts involving sex. However, during the 16th century in England, the upper social classes developed an administrative approach for themselves by way of the Court of High Commission. Functioning from 1558 to 1640, this court dealt with unusual sexual and family practices. Persons committing acts such as adultery, incest, bigamy, immorality, assault with intent to ravish, swearing desperate oaths, and blasphemy were handled by these two parallel bodies: the system of ecclesiastical courts and the High Commission. Assignment was determined in part by the offender's economic and social rank. Contrary to what might be expected, the penalties assessed by the High Commission were sometimes more severe than those assessed by the ecclesiastical courts for similar offenses. By the time of the Puritan ascendancy and the English Civil War in the middle of the 17th century, when the English monarchy was abolished, both ecclesiastical jurisdiction and the High Commission had fallen into disuse. Although the former was restored along with the monarchy in 1660, the period of existence without such devices had demonstrated a lack of need.

Over the centuries, either by creation of specific statutes or common law assumption of general jurisdiction, the common law courts gradually took charge of offenses within the domain of marital and sexual aberration. In the reign of Henry VIII (1507-1547) a specific statute was created to deal with "unnatural offenses." As one index of behavior believed to need legal regulation at the time, bigamy became a crime in 1603. The influence of the ecclesiastical courts lingered in England by way of their retention of jurisdiction over divorces until 1857 when special "divorce courts" were created. Over the last century in England various sexual offenses acts were enacted based on different aims that were often in conflict, such as prohibiting sexual acts believed immoral by way of the criminal law even though the utilitarian goal of preventing demonstrable harm was not in question.

Medley of sex enactments

Without laboring further the course in England, it can be pointed out that the sex laws that emerged consisted of a medley of enactments from many historical periods. These were often couched in quaint language and perhaps imposed maximum penalties that had little connection either with the harmfulness or prevalence of a particular offense. Historical surveys point out the haphazard manner in which sexual acts have been incorporated into the criminal law to serve a variety of purposes, not only in England but also in the United States and most other countries. For example, in England intercourse *per anum* by a man with his wife (buggery) is still subject to life imprisonment while the same act between two males in private is not a crime.[2] However, at least England has been free of the special types of sex statutes that emerged in the United States providing for different rules for commitment, detainment, treatment, and release.

In colonial America, fornication and "lewd and lascivious" or "wanton behaviors" were the most frequently punished sexual offenses. Since these terms lacked precise meaning, they were applied as required.[3] Behaviors such as prostitution, abduction, or certain sexual dalliances were also forbidden. "Treatment" ideas were tied to "bodily punishment" (e.g., public whippings in the market place where half of them took place). Ideas of punishment to prevent recurrence of individual sexual transgressions were fused with ideas of deterring others. Within the group of "sexual transgressors," about three-fourths were fornicators and usually included the younger people in the population.[4] Such data are probably similar to what would be obtained today if such an enforcement were to take place. Current studies indicate that the largest percent of increase in nonvirginal adult women may actually have occurred 50 years ago, with the proportion resting at about 50 percent since the 1920s.[5] The rate may be increasing since, according to one national survey, 46 percent of all unmarried women in the United States have engaged in sexual intercourse by age 19.[6] However, no one argues that these figures were approached during colonial times.

Colonial Massachusetts during the 17th century can be

taken as a prototype for illustration—subject to local variation in colonies where the Puritan ethic was not thriving with
pristine vigor. In early colonial days and continuing up to the
late 18th century, Puritan criminal law was heavily infused
with Mosaic law. Sin and crime tended to be equated, and
hence the sinner was a criminal. Criminal law was the worldly
application of the law of God. No separate ecclesiastical
courts were required because religious notions involving sex
were incorporated into the application of the civil law. In a
broad sense, the primary goal of criminal law was the enforcement of the morals and religion of the people. Not until
the post-revolutionary period did the goals shift to the protection of property and physical security.

Whippings administered to secure reform were not paltry
affairs. These punishments were carried out in the stern
conviction that they were being administered with the ultimate goal of reforming wayward persons. By way of excluding sadistic elements, specific directions were given to set
limits on the selection of those administering such punishments. Hence, no one who was "cruel or barbarous" would
be permitted to do the whipping, and the number of lashes
to be "laid on" was specified—usually 15 or 20. Even a "detestable offense" did not get more than the Biblical, 39, citing
the authority of Paul's "second letter to the Corinthians."
Whipping was also the chosen punishment for adulterers
and for girls who delivered illegitimate children.

Rape becomes a capital offense

In the 1640s buggery with man or beast was punishable by
death for either participant. The offending animal might be
executed before the eyes of the guilty person, supposedly to
cleanse them both. Scriptural authority was cited for such
action. In fact, Old Testament language is still used, as witnessed in the current statutory definition of sodomy in Massachusetts as ". . . the abominable and detestable crime

against nature either with mankind or with a beast."[7] For a
time there was a hesitancy to inflict capital punishment without scriptural authority. In the 1641 "Body of Liberties" of
the Massachusetts Bay Colony, rape was not a capital offense,
but by 1648 it had become one. It was the only capital offense
to be listed without a Biblical citation to justify the punishment.[8] Adultery with a married or espoused woman was a
capital crime for both parties. Sexual intercourse between a
married man and a single unbetrothed woman, however,
was considered to be no more than fornication.

In the 18th century provincial government of Massachusetts, subsequent to colonial times but prior to the Rev-
olution, treatment measures were lightened somewhat, but
their essential character did not change. Consideration of
some of the specific offenses and how they were handled
illustrates this. Fornication with a single female became
punishable by ten stripes or a fine of five pounds. Adultery in
colonial times, as noted, was a capital offense punishable by
death if it involved married or espoused women. From 1692
to 1780 adultery became punishable by 40 lashes and sitting
in the gallows for one hour with a rope around the neck to
impress upon the culprit that his behavior was "deadly seri-
ousness." Thereafter, the guilty parties were required to
wear a two-inch high letter "A" visible upon their clothing for
the remainder of their lives. A convicted adulterer found
without it was subject to 15 lashes. The scarlet letter worn by
Hester Prynne in Nathaniel Hawthorne's famous novel pro-
claimed her an adulteress.[9] Incestuous marriages were subject
to the same penalty as adultery except that the letter "I" was
to be worn for life. Transvestite behavior was handled by
corporal punishment or a fine of up to five pounds.

Punishment for rape varied with class

The unfolding history of how rape was handled in English
law is intriguing. The impression left is that sexually assaul-

tive behavior against "propertied virgins" met with severe penalties. The reason for this was that one's wife and children were personal property, and it was never quite resolved as to whether rape was a crime against a woman's body or against an estate.[10] Bracton stated that prior to the Norman Conquest in 1066, the penalty for raping this class of women was death and dismemberment (including the loss of the scrotum and the tails of the rapist's horse and dog).[11] The female victim would be given the male's land and money although she could spare the execution of her ravisher by marrying him.

After the Norman Conquest the mode of trial shifted from ordeal to combat. A finding of guilt resulted in castration and perhaps blinding. If a woman had no champion to fight her cause, the accused won his case. A century later jury trial had replaced combat. Bracton did not even bother to discuss the rape of propertied "nonvirgins" since such behavior in this class of females was not yet viewed as sufficiently serious to involve the Crown. Such offenses were still handled through manorial courts with "chastisement falling short of loss of limb" to the male. Further, rape of the whole class of "unpropertied virgins" appears to have been handled haphazardly, although in the 13th century the manorial courts were dealing with these as well.

By the end of the 13th century the Statutes of Westminster (A.D. 1275 and 1285, respectively) extended the jurisdiction of the Crown to cover forcible rape of all women with no difference in punishment between offenders.[12] The significance of this was that rape then became a public crime in contrast to a matter for the local manors. The escape hatch of allowing the victim to marry the perpetrator was eliminated, and the principle of statutory rape for minors was established. The First Statute of Westminster made the sentence for rape two years' imprisonment and perhaps a fine; in A.D. 1285 the statute was amended to make rape a felony punishable by death. Little has changed since then, and this heritage was brought to America. Throughout, the behavior was not viewed as a reflection of a disturbed personality but rather predatory behavior like other aggressive acts of taking which the criminal law regulated.

In colonial times in America rape was punishable by death once the lack of a warrant for this penalty in the Holy Scriptures was ignored. Originally, the most severe penalty short of death was meted out when the victim was a minor. This might consist of the maximum number of lashings permitted, but it might also mean slitting the offender's nostrils or condemning him never to appear in public thereafter without a halter about his neck. Statutes were enacted making statutory rape punishable by death although in practice the lives of most transgressors were spared.

"Aggravated rape" offenders were usually required to continue wearing a rope around the neck. During the 19th century, the rape of a woman or carnal knowledge of a child under age 10 continued to be punishable by death. Sodomy and bestiality were viewed as behavior "contrary to the light of nature," again relying upon the Biblical injunction that "mankinde lyeth with mankinde." These offenses were punishable by death unless the perpetrator was under the age of 14, although by 1805 these acts had been removed from the list of capital offenses.[13]

Colonies on the expanding frontier varied in their manner of dealing with sex offenders. Throughout the 19th and 20th centuries, state laws emerged which superseded common law practices by way of codification of criminal behavior. These statutes began to include classifications of sexual offenses as part of the criminal code. It was not considered necessary to treat sexual behavior any differently from other acts defined as criminal. Accordingly, disposition was made in the same manner as for other criminal acts and was subject to the same available defenses. Some offenders were found incompetent to stand trial, others occasionally pled insanity when some major offense involving sexual violence occurred, and still others were handled civilly as being mentally ill and a final disposition postponed indefinitely.

3

EVOLUTION OF SEX OFFENDER STATUTES

In terms of dealing with sex offenders, the modern era was heralded by the legislative approach of enacting special "sexual psychopath" statutes in the late 1930s. As we have noted, this was a manifestation of a political-legislative approach to a community problem, but it infused jargon from the psychiatric field as well. Anxiety about sexual crimes, particularly those having violent overtones or involving children, often created the atmosphere for the passage of such legislation. The primary goal of public protection from threatening sexual behavior remained.

By the 20th century, the public had become increasingly concerned about brutal sex offenses as more sophisticated mass media made widespread publicity of these crimes possible. In addition, the mass media aroused public awareness of psychoanalysis and sexuality in an uninformed manner. The comforting but misleading impression grew that most types of sexual deviance should be dealt with by treatment, voluntarily or not.

In time, pessimism about the deterrent effects of incapacitation in institutions for sexual crimes *per se* gave way to a pessimism, equally deep, about the ineffectiveness or inadequacy of the type of treatment provided, or the lack of treatment altogether, during the period of confinement. Early and unjustified optimism had raised public hopes about the effectiveness of clinical approaches in identifying and predicting just who would behave in a deviant or dangerous manner. Intimately fused with the belief in the ability of clinicians to identify and predict sexual psychopathy for the legal system was the illusion that treatments were available to cure and rehabilitate the individuals identified. Accordingly, administration of the sex statutes was geared to the objectives of incapacitation, treatment, and prevention.

Evaluation problems persist

The complex clinical problem of evaluating myriad lines of sexual maldevelopment has persisted. Methodologic handicaps have permeated most research, making conclusions about treatment results very tentative. Studies done with those confined always pose special problems for evaluating behavior on release. The variety among those treated as sexual offenders has resulted in mixing disparate groups, thus compounding the complexity of validating any research. A fluctuating zealousness associated with certain rehabilitative approaches that became fashionable set a predictable pattern: Whatever treatment was fashionable at a given time would be suggested as the cure to be used for sex offenders. Validation of the treatment modality in question relied more often than not upon short-term follow-ups with unsophisticated assessment of personality. Optimistic claims for any one particular treatment of sex offenders remains highly suspect. Humane compassion for those institutionalized as sex offenders often has not been distinguished from the need for valid and reliable criteria to evaluate therapeutic procedures.

Conflict has arisen both on theoretical grounds and in administrative decision-making for dealing with those who are judicially classified as sex offenders. Selected problems with mixed clinical-legal significance will be used to illustrate several key issues. Consider the supposedly simple problem of the mental examination of a sex offender. Statutes in different states vary in matters such as when the examination will be performed. Examinations may be done prior to a hearing on the alleged sexual behavior in question (if no crime has been committed) or not until just prior to sentencing. In addition, there is variation between optional and mandatory requirements for a mental examination to be performed. The same behavior, with the same conviction, in a different state might require an examination, but the state might not have the capability of carrying it out. Such discrepancies are comparable to the variation in sentencing procedures.

Variation also exists as to which offenses require such examinations and where and how they will be performed. The purpose of the "mental examination" may not be specified. In practice some are used simply to provide additional facts to a court prior to sentencing. However, there is usually an implication in most of the statutes that the psychiatrist will tell the court whether a given defendant should be treated as a patient or sentenced as a criminal. Such examinations are often expected to yield a recommendation as to whether some type of "specialized" treatment (the nature of which usually remains unspecified) should be ordered as an alternative to a prison sentence. This use of a psychiatrist permits courts to justify their sentences whether the sex offender is sent to a prison or is held in some type of special treatment facility. Facilities frequently carry labels such as the "hospital for the criminally insane," or "state security hospital." Some states locate their treatment facilities in separate parts of state prisons while others designate a wing of a particular state hospital.

Another group of problems arises from the civil rather than criminal nature of the commitment process for sex psychopaths. Opportunities can and do arise for an accused or convicted sex offender to contest the findings of a mental health examiner. Qualifications for the examiner are often vague and undefined. Similarly, the criteria for committing someone as a sex deviant and detaining him for "special treatment" are vague. Charges of violating due process may arise when a person is so classified on the basis of an uncontestable and unanswerable determination made by some welfare department examiner. Thus, in one case the defendant was found not only to have the right to a special hearing and to cross-examine his examiners but also the right to be examined by a psychiatrist or other physician of his own choosing, the right to subpoena and cross-examine witnesses, and the right to counsel.[14]

Statutes ambiguous

Questions related to clinical evaluations performed under the aegis of sex statutes continue to arise. As noted, parts of statutes are ambiguous. The qualifications of the mental health examiner who will do the examining may not be specified, or the statute may simply specify that the examiner be a physician. In some communities these are family physicians or public health officials who have had minimal exposure to clinical aspects of sexual psychopathology apart from a few lectures or films. A "psychiatrist" specified as the examiner may in practice mean anyone listed as a specialist in mental illness without reference to specific postgraduate training criteria. If the sex offender is a juvenile, the examination is often carried out by an examiner who has no special qualifications for assessment of juveniles. Examinations may be performed by trainees (such as residents) in various medical centers. Whether this level of training sufficiently protects a person's rights can be challenged when loss of liberty is a possible outcome. The same stricture holds for Ph.D. candidates in training centers when their recommendations can result in an indeterminate commitment for special treatment as a sex offender.

The lack of standards used to evaluate submitted reports

raises another series of complex issues. In many cases no elaboration of the reasoning processes and inferences is offered. Evaluations may simply consist of conclusions and recommendations, a practice comparable to the worst use of experts in other areas of concern to the law and psychiatry, such as in providing summary answers to questions. Requiring affirmative or negative answers to certain questions (e.g., is a given individual a sexual psychopath or is he in need of treatment) often lead to arbitrary and unsubstantiated opinions. They represent examples of psychiatry and law at their lowest level.

The various sex statutes have often incorporated unclarified clinical assumptions, with the actual bases used for dispositional recommendations by clinicians either not known or not mentioned. Recommendations that an individual be treated as a sex offender may be based primarily on the fact that he has first been indicted and/or convicted of a sex crime. On that antecedent basis a clinician then decides whether a prisoner should be labeled and handled as a sex offender. The key question is whether there is some independent basis in a psychiatric examination for determining when an individual should be handled as a sex offender, under special legal provisions, rather than as a convicted criminal. The assumption that the psychiatrist is able to make this differentiation is doubted by many. The question is whether the psychiatrist's conclusions have any greater validity for disposition than some other approach (such as actuarial data), but what remains important is to articulate the basis for the difference.

Available treatments vary

The modalities of treatment actually available in a given state and locality vary widely. What is supposed to be available may bear little resemblance to what is really offered. Psychiatrists and judges may have little first hand knowledge of these vital matters. The qualifications of professional personnel in the institutions to which sex offenders are sent for treatment also bear some relevance to the purposes of a statute that allows people to be sent to such institutions. The statutes emerged as a protective device. If the treatment provided is perfunctory or capricious, that fact should be made known. The problem is how to enlighten psychiatrists, judges, attorneys, legislators, and the general public about how oppressive and inadequate the system is. (That topic is discussed further in Chapters 5 and 11.)

Administrative practices involved in the application of sex offender statutes raise a different set of policy questions. One group of problems involves the practice of administrators, rather than professional clinicians, determining relative dispositions of individuals convicted of sexual offenses once they are within the system. These decision-making processes have a low visibility and are characterized and accompanied by a minimum of clinical participation. A related problem is whether or not sentencing decisions for a given individual should be subject to an adversary process, which would allow debate about alternatives and prognoses and perhaps make the stage of disposition as adversarial as a trial.

Such debates would make the risks involved in treatment or rehabilitation processes more available to public scrutiny. Criticisms that certain judges, psychiatrists, and "treaters" on a given case are either too permissive or too harsh could increase as a consequence of greater visibility. A frequent administrative practice is to place those legally designated as "sex offenders" in types of special "hospitals." It has been argued that they should be placed instead in ordinary mental institutions with other civilly committed patients and, thenceforth, be handled by clinicians as are other patients. Determination of treatment, what kind, and how much, are often decisions that tax the most sophisticated clinicians. Yet, in institutions for sex offenders treatment may be carried out with a mixture of goals and practices. The overriding concern is community safety subsequent to release, despite the difficulty of prediction. Such concern for community safety is similar to decisions to release prisoners on parole, with the difference that many are released from prison whether considered dangerous or not when their sentences have expired. To reiterate, no special qualifications are usually required for those who treat sex offenders. The ultimate questions are what level of qualification is necessary to achieve treatment goals for committed sex offenders and who is willing to pay for it? The answers hinge partially on whether or not the public wants its institutions to be more than custodial or penal residences.

The question of "dangerousness"

The issue of "dangerousness" often remains controlling in terms of the ongoing commitment status of the sex offender, as well as his readiness for release. It is deceptive to say that courts make independent decisions since this avoids clarification of who contributes to the decision-making. The role of a psychiatrist may be confined simply to giving an *opinion* whether a certain defendant is dangerous. However, in some situations and jurisdictions psychiatrists influence the actual *criteria* used in determination of dangerousness. Some persons involved in the review process might view exhibitionism accompanied by obscene threats as dangerous to the public in a certain social or moral sense, while a psychiatrist might not consider these criteria controlling in evaluating dangerousness. Hence, "dangerousness" is viewed as a legal concept by some, while others view it as a clinical concept. Yet it may also be viewed as an expression of public policy about behavior. A basic issue is the lack of clinical validity for the legal concept of "sexually dangerous." The combined legal-psychiatric machinery for handling those persons alleged to be sexually dangerous then becomes a *de facto* method of practicing preventive detention to hold them out of society for an indeterminate period.

An even more serious problem connected with the emergence of sex psychopath statutes is the fusion of the assumption of criminal responsibility with the determination of sexual psychopathy as a justification for disposition. An evaluation of a sex offender may reach a conclusion that at the time of committing a rape a person was not able to conform his conduct to the requirements of the law, or that he could not control himself, or that his act was the product of his sexual psychopathy. Not only are mixed concepts being employed, but concepts regarding criminal responsibility for behavior are utilized while an insanity defense is bypassed at trial. Attempts to answer many of these questions reveal how inadequate and deplorable our current approach to people who are convicted of sex crimes actually is.

It is further important to realize that an implicit assumption of sex psychopath statutes is that an individual is criminally responsible for his behavior. The states with sex psychopath statutes that permit an individual to be committed as a sex psychopath without a sex crime ever having been committed have an assumption that the person would be held criminally responsible for his behavior *if* it ever did occur. On the other hand, it is possible that such an individual might be found not guilty at a trial if such a crime did occur. This is analogous to finding someone legally insane without first finding him guilty of the acts. In this ambiguous world, both society and the individual suffer.

4
STATUTORY CRITERIA FOR IDENTIFICATION OF SEX PSYCHOPATHS

Examination of the laws of some 28 jurisdictions that have sex offender statutes reveals different but overlapping criteria for commitment.[15] These criteria can be summarized into seven features that are used for identification of sex offenders:

(1) *Commission of a sexual offense—It is usually specified that sexual misconduct and/or a sexual criminal offense has either taken place and has been followed by conviction or a plea of guilty before specific statutory provisions are invoked.* However, as noted, this is not a criterion held to by all states since some statutes permit a standard based on the possibility that such a course of misconduct or offense *will* occur in the foreseeable future. Some statutes itemize the criminal offenses that will specifically qualify (e.g., rape, sodomy, incest, etc.), but others simply state that any sex crime suffices. Frequently, the general term "public offense" is used, which permits identification of a sex offender who thereby becomes involved in the intricacies of the statute.

The sexual offenses most frequently singled out in statutes are those accompanied by physical force or violence and acts of sexual assault or sexual molestation of children. However, note that the first sex psychopath statute to withstand constitutional attack did not require conviction for a sex crime for a person to be committed. A Minnesota statute simply required a committing court to be persuaded that the person accused met the definition of a sex psychopath. The presumption was that on the basis of an examination by physicians, not necessarily psychiatrists, a determination of a "psychopathic personality" could be reached. Such a personality was defined as "the existence in any person of such conditions of emotional instability, or impulsiveness of behavior, or lack of customary standards of good judgment or failure to appreciate the consequences of his acts, or a combination of any such conditions as to render such person irresponsible for his conduct with respect to sexual matters and thereby dangerous to other persons."[16] The constitutionality of this statute was upheld by the United States Supreme Court in 1940.[17] A similar meaning has been retained in all of the subsequent statutes that attempted to designate such a group. For example, the District of Columbia defined a "sexual psychopath" as ". . . a person, not insane, who by a course of repeated misconduct in sexual matters has evidenced such lack of power to control his sexual impulses as to be dangerous to other persons because he is likely to attack or otherwise inflict injury, loss, pain, or other evil on the objects of his desire."[18]

(2) *Sexually dangerous act—Emphasis is given in sexual offenses legislation to the underlying public belief that these acts carry an especially high risk of dangerous behavior.* The special attention carries the implication that criminal sexual conduct is inherently more dangerous than other criminal behavior. Hence, sexual psychopaths would be seen as more dangerous individuals than criminals. Although physical danger to a person is frequently connoted by inclusion of such terms as "physical force or violence," physical aggression is more frequently stressed. Psychological damage to the victim is included in the concept of a menace or danger emanating from "sexually dangerous" acts. The concept of danger is always implicit, and is often explicit, for sexual acts involving legal minors or children.

(3) *Repetition of an offense—Almost all of the statutes carry phrases that characterize the offender as one who repeats his sexual misconduct or offensive behavior or who is likely to repeat it in the foreseeable future.* Some use the phrase "habitual," but more often the connotation is implied. There is usually no need to establish a pattern as a "recidivistic offender" in order to be identified for the purpose of most sex offender legislation.

(4) *Risk of future community danger—Related to the foregoing, and most important as a primary issue for identification purposes, are terms that denote an assumed high probability of future risk.* All statutes carry this inference of a high likelihood that such misconduct will occur and that a reliable prediction can be made about such future acts. Sex offender legislation that differentially segregates one sex offender from another is based upon the assumption that it is possible to reliably identify the individual who has a high risk of sexual offending in the foreseeable future from lower risk persons. "High risk" rather than "low risk" is always implied, if not specified, within the statutes. Again, it may have been that some statutes had in mind separating the "one shot" offender from his more habitual counterpart.

Statutes use language such as "persons who are predisposed to sexual offenses," have "criminal propensities," are a "menace to the public," who "lack control over their impulses," or are "likely to attack or inflict injury, loss, pain, or evil on others." Many statutes conceptualize this predictive feature by specifying that the civil commitment of the offender is a legal means of protecting the community. A sex psychopath or a sex offender is then incapacitated until he is safe to be returned to society or is no longer considered to have a dangerous potential. It is often underscored that this involuntary hospitalization is to be clearly differentiated and not to be viewed as punishment for sexual misconduct.

Criteria for release of sex offenders also involve predictions of future risk of dangerousness. These are in the same confused state as for other civilly or criminally committed persons generally. Since release decisions are often made by a host of low visibility processes, the specific criteria relied on are seldom evident. The question arises as to whether many of these decisions are being made primarily on a descriptive level, such as by observations based on the externals of behavior while institutionalized, conformity toward norms, or performance at parole hearings. In reality, these criteria have as little predictive validity regarding sexual behavior after release from a security institution as they do for predicting criminal behavior. The problem related to overprediction of dangerousness poses the threat of many "false positives" who are kept institutionalized when they could be released into the community. If they are released, they become a problem of community monitoring where we have little experience but much anxiety about implementation.

Statutory itemization of character traits of the sex offender or sex psychopath assumes that such traits imply a supposed predictability about future behavior. Personality traits listed as part of the picture of a "sexual psychopath" (e.g., emotional instability or impulsiveness of behavior) connote a high risk of offending in the foreseeable future. More recent statutes, or amendments to old ones, omit or delete specific reference to these terms, albeit stressing in other ways the high risk of recurrence of such sexual misconduct or offenses.

Rarely are predictive criteria specified by statute or case law. There is a general unrealistic expectation that the psychiatrist is competent to make accurate long-term predictions of sexual misconduct. Nor do psychiatric signs and symptoms establish predictive criteria for dangerousness. As a final caveat, it should not be assumed that some other satisfactory bases for prediction exist. In some jurisdictions, many sex offenders so identified are first time offenders. Predictions of high risk are supposedly to be made from "other," independent clinical data. Repeated sex offending or misconduct is a significant behavioral index on the level of its indication of repetitiveness. However, psychiatric expertise is not required to reach a conclusion of recidivism when several acts have already occurred. High level research has obviously been needed for a long time to determine whether reliable prediction indices can be developed. Such research, though sorely needed, is uniformly accorded very low funding priority by public agencies. We do not believe that any such reliable and valid instrument exists at present. Although it is assumed that psychiatric skill is adequate for reliable prediction purposes, the absence, in fact, of such skill, along with similar unreliability in psychometric devices, is one of the most severe criticisms of special sex psychopath legislation and the failure of its implementation in legal and psychiatric practice.

(5) *Community protection—All of the statutes, either explicitly or implicity, express the concept that sexually dangerous persons pose such a threat to a community that special security measures and indeterminate commitment are needed for protection.* The aura of imminent threat surrounding the sex offender classification is often considered exaggerated and excessive by many mental health professionals. However, this standard is basic to all special sex psychopath legislation. Many questions arise with respect to whether or not community protection is in fact secured by these statutes or whether the statutes are actually misguided attempts at community reassurance against dangers that do not exist.

(6) *Mental illness or defect—The presence of mental illness, mental disorder, or mental deficiency in the sex offender is another feature used in statutes to identify the sex offender.* The term mental illness thus used is often implied in these statutes in a broad sense that includes many types of character disorders. Thus, a statute may require that the actor be identified as mentally ill but without specifying anything further in a diagnostic sense. "Psychopathic personality" is the most fre-

quently encountered diagnostic category mentioned in statutes, although some do not go beyond the description "mentally disordered sex offender."

The distinction between psychiatric diagnosis and the
terms used in sex psychopath statutes, and their lack of
equivalence, is important. Frequently included in the definition are terms causally relating sexual misconduct or offense
to mental illness or disorder by such definitive phrases as "[if
the actor] suffers from any form of abnormal or subnormal
mental illness, or other psychosis, which caused the commission of the sex offense." More frequently the term "predis-
position" is used to confer a causal relationship between the
mental disorder of deficiency and the sexual behavior. Frequently, the causal relationship is implicit, and the mere
presence of mental illness in the actor or offender is seen as
defining the mentally ill sex offender.

Such a broad definition of mental illness in the sex
psychopath statutes allows almost any mental aberration or
emotional disorder to qualify. The process can be inferential
or can actually be demonstrated by behavior. Such breadth
of scope and latitude in definition of mental illness allows
almost any person to be defined as mentally ill if he concomitantly possesses some of the other identifying features.
The absence of rigorous diagnostic criteria, as employed by
competent psychiatrists in their professional work, makes a
mockery of attempts to justify dispositions of such persons
on a clinical basis.

The problem of the reliability of diagnoses is sufficiently
great in psychiatry itself apart from how sex psychopath
statutes use the concept of mental illness. The circularity of
this relationship is repeatedly demonstrated by identifying
the special sex offender on the basis of minimal evidence of
psychopathology and instead inferring mental illness from
the act itself. Worse yet, some type of divergent state of mind
may be predicated and then used to fulfill statutory criteria.

Support for the identification of inferred mental illness is made on the basis that the act in question occurred. More frequently than not, mental illness is deduced primarily, if not solely, from the commission of the sexually deviant act, misconduct, or offense. Circular reasoning is manifested in the act's defining mental illness and mental illness, in turn, being defined by the act.

(7) *Treatability of designated sex offenders—Many statutes include the concept of the need for treatment once the offender has been segregated.* Treatability, as such, however, is rarely included as a necessary condition for identification of the sex offender. Further comments about treatability and the right to receive adequate treatment are important and are discussed later in Chapter 11. Identification of the sex offender is determined more by the criterion of his dangerousness to the community than by his need or response to treatment, which might not reduce his potential dangerousness. Treatment phrases and terms included in the definition of the sex offender relate to some type of implied or acknowledged causal relationship between mental illness and sexual misconduct or offenses. Beyond this is the implication as well that successful treatment of the offender will reduce the probability of future sexual offenses and, hence, his dangerousness.

Psychiatric criticism of special sex psychopath legislation is frequently directed to these types of deficits in definitions. The absence of a valid diagnostic framework, lack of standardization of assessments, low accuracy of prognostic statements, wide divergencies in the quality of evaluators, and the limitations of treatment all contribute to the confusion. There is uncertainty about the uniform need for treatment of the sexual psychopath, the likelihood of his satisfactory response to it, and the availability and effective application of accepted treatment modalities for the institutionalized offender.

5

METHODOLOGICAL PROBLEMS IN EVALUATING TREATMENT

Given the heterogeneous population legally categorized as sex offenders, it is not surprising that reliable conclusions about the efficacy of treatment are most difficult to reach. This is not to ignore the impassioned claims, past and present, for some particular therapeutic approach to which therapists have been exposed or which appeals to them based on a multitude of personal preferences. It does mean that major factors of credibility exist when dispassionate assessments of results are made. There are many reasons that vitiate the claims made for any particular treatment programs. As noted, a population of sex offenders is taken from a *legal* grouping that has no particular clinical significance in terms of their alleged psychopathology. Reports of treatment results based on groups of "sex psychopaths," "rapists," or those found guilty of some degree of "criminal sexual conduct" have limited psychiatric application. It follows, therefor, that establishing comparable control groups, with similar signs, symptoms, and socio-cultural factors, is difficult if not impossible. Sole reliance on legal categories, such as rape, for division into control and treated groups is not a sufficiently valid basis to evaluate treatment results.

Another problem pertains to the small size of the populations on which treatment procedures are carried out. In a statistical sense there is also the problem of behaviors with a low base rate in which prediction is quite unreliable. The pervasive problem of evaluating any kind of treatment carried out in the context of a security institution has major limitations. It is not a setting where an individual can adequately test the success of any personality change related to sexual behavior. If community follow-up is attempted, the criteria used to measure success are often based on factors such as not getting into difficulties in their communities or on rates of recidivism, hardly reliable standards based on the innumerable criminal acts that occur and that do not receive official recognition. Prominent among these would be rape and pedophila, which are underreported.

Few studies define what "cure" or successful treatment of sexual offenders means. Do we mean a clinical cure, and, if so, in terms of what? In fact, on the basis of subsequent sexual offenses (recidivism rates), treated and untreated groups do not appear to differ.[19] Some argue that there are certain treatment approaches that may actually be harmful, but the same type of critique should be applied to these advocates as well as to those who tell us how successful their approaches are. The same canon of scientific investigation should hold for both. While many interesting, innovative, or "common sense" approaches have been urged, most have many major limitations. Simply providing for a fine or some *ad hoc* shaming device, such as being put in the stocks, might prove as effective on some outcome measures as any other device.[20] Again, it depends on the measure used. Most, if not all, of the treatments offered for sex offenders can be considered "experimental." If the criterion for experimental is that the procedures are not clearly established as beneficial by clinical experience or scientific standards, if is not difficult to take such a position.

The entire spectrum of therapies used and advocated for sex offenders cannot be discussed in this report. What we wish to do is provide a critique for evaluation of the confusion present in treatment techniques applied to sexual offenders. Hopefully, a result will be to minimize future confusion.

Assessment of treatment difficult

It is very difficult to assess the effectiveness of treatment based upon what society or professionals would judge to be a severe offense. At one time successful treatment was considered possible only in those who had committed minor misdemeanor types of offenses such as voyeurism or exhibitionism. However, we now know that some of these patients are as difficult to treat as others who display more offensive behavior. Even if a criterion based solely on eliminating a specific symptom is used, minor sexually offensive behavior may be as resistant to change as other more disturbing sexual behavior. If we employ additional criteria (e.g., altering troublesome social or personal behavior) we are setting the standards for effectiveness much higher.

At one time, pedophilia was thought to be highly treatable; in retrospect, this optimism appears to have confused social policy needs with actual therapeutic effectiveness. There are certain sexual offenders—as divergent as homosexual pedophiles compared to rapists of adult females—who may join in an alliance with a therapist and respond better than others whose offenses are less flamboyant. Again, the problem arises of evaluation in terms of legal categories. For example, treatment might be more difficult with a compulsive voyeur whose behavior is a secondary symptom of refractory schizophrenia than treatment of a rapist who is responding to a marital situation that has deteriorated and may be remediable. Note the confusion that results in evaluating outcome in terms of recidivism when clinical inquiry is made that is quite different than "criminological" indices relying on previous records.

The problem of base rates has been mentioned. Applied to the clinical problem of treatment, the base rate is the expected rate of recidivism in the absence of treatment. Even these criteria are complicated by the difficulties related to the number of complaints, apprehension, public visibility of the offense, official processing, and so on. It is important to know, for example, that few sexual criminals recidivate with a new sexual crime. In one study analyzing recidivism rates for 2,934 male sexual criminals, re-examined up to 24 years after initial conviction, the recidivism rate was only 10 percent for new sex crimes.[21] First offenders had a recidivism rate of only 6.9 percent for new sex offenses.

The importance of these findings is that unless sex statutes do, in fact, only screen repetitive offenders, which may not be the case, "treatment" results would be expected to be good merely as a function of the base rates for the offenders in question. Persons with a prior history of recidivistic sexual offenses repeated at a rate of 23 percent for new sexual offenses; persons whose prior history consisted of mixed property and sexual offenses recidivated at a rate of 25 percent for new sex offenses and had a total recidivism rate of 45 percent. Recidivism involving the same kind of sexual behavior is most likely with indecency toward children and exhibitionism.[22] This finding correlates with one of the major societal concerns—aggressive sexual acts against children. The general recidivism rate for convicted sexual offenders in court populations is low, lying between 13 and 17 percent. Exhibitionism and homosexual pedophilia have the highest rates of about 20 to 30 percent. Previous criminal records also affect behavioral predictions. Offenders with previous sexual convictions are about three times more likely to commit another offense than first offenders.[23]

These findings are significant because there are few reports that enable anyone to make valid statements about the effects of differential treatments among heterogeneous groups who come within the boundaries of sex laws. Given the present difficulties of treatment evaluations coupled with good prognoses of first offenders, it would be difficult to argue for any type of "coercive" treatment for such persons. Neither the treatment nor the need for treatment is established. The more serious behaviors are fortunately less recidivistic; the less serious sexual behaviors have a correlative degree of less public concern but are those with high base rates. As a result, they would be the easiest group on which to establish the actual effect of any treatment procedure.

Studies raise doubts about treatment efficacy

Some studies raise serious doubts about the efficacy of what is called "treatment." Studies from California found that a sample of sex offenders paroled from a California state hospital had a five year cumulative recidivism rate of 26.6 percent, slightly below that of sex offenders paroled from California prisons.[24] On breaking down the categories by types of deviancy among the patients, it was found that there was a considerable variation in recidivism rates among groups, with approximately 10 percent recidivism for patients with daughter or step-daughter victims versus about 47 percent for patients convicted of voyeurism, transvestism, and lewd behavior.[25]

Criminal variables, such as the type of offense committed or the age of the offender, rather than mental health variables *per se*, appear to be a predominant influence in determining the outcome of treatment. A research group in Massachusetts has, however, claimed that dangerousness in sex offenders is diagnosable and treatable.[26] Dangerous sex offenders were treated for an average period of 43 months and then released. These persons were reported as committing new serious assaults at a rate of only 6.1 percent. This figure is compared to a new serious crime rate of 34.7 percent among patients released by court order against the advice of the clinical staff. However, despite the enthusiasm engendered by the foregoing study, considerable methodologic inadequacies compromise its interpretation.[27] Another study

from Massachusetts reported a high degree of success in the
outpatient mental health treatment of exhibitionists, but with
failure most evident among a small group of the most aggressive.[28] However, most states do not even classify
exhibitionism in the category of felonious sexual behavior—
an example of how a group perhaps amenable to treatment
evokes least community concern. Nevertheless, it does not
suffice merely to know that certain sex offenders are "treatable" or even that the criminal aspects of a sexual act are seen
as products of a mental disorder. To justify the types of sex
psychopath laws in existence requires evidence that sex offenders whose behavior is both "dangerous" and repetitive
are treatable. Without this, the justification for their special
processing outside the usual provisions of the criminal justice
system is lacking.

Many caveats must be kept in mind when considering
treatment as part of the legal disposition for sex offenders. If
these are not heeded, the kind of situation existing among
states with sex offender statutes is uncritically perpetuated.
Fallacious thinking about recidivism due to the base rate
problem is only one example. Another relates to programs
developed on the basis of viewing sex offenders as a
homogeneous group. Nor is this homogeneity fallacy restricted to legal categorization. For example, a simplistic
psychodynamic framework hypothesizes that "sex offenders"
behave antisocially in an attempt to lessen anxiety. Paradoxi-
cally, such a psychodynamic formulation becomes twisted.
The result is then the same as that advocated by the clinically
unsophisticated, i.e., since diverse behaviors that are sexually
offensive are attempts to cope with or lessen anxiety, it is not
necessary to seek out more specific etiologies or alternative
psychodynamic models to explain the diverse acts in question. When it comes to public understanding of our meager
knowledge about sexual psychopathology a little learning is a
dangerous thing.

6

THE DOCTRINE OF INFORMED CONSENT RELATED TO THE TREATMENT OF SEX OFFENDERS

Many factors virtually guarantee that the confined sex offender will be exposed to significant risks at some point during his "rehabilitation." Selected by often vague statutory criteria, he shares with other sex offenders no common etiology for his presumed psychopathology. Yet he is restrained in the face of a social ambivalence that demands "treatment" for his "illness" while simultaneously condoning punishment and stigma as an expression of public outrage and fear concerning criminal sexual behavior. It comes as no surprise that much of the "treatment" offered sex offenders is experimental in nature. Many studies seeking to define the effectiveness of psychiatric treatments for sex offenders seem notable for their lack of rigorous experimental design, for statistical fallacies, and even for experimenter biases.

If the confined sex offender were exposed only to low-risk treatment modalities for his condition, there might be little need for concern about potentially adverse results. But the treatments in question are more appropriately viewed along a continuum extending from benign "milieu" therapies to the most dramatic, somatic, and even irreversible interventions such as psychosurgery. (Along the way from least to most severe interventions one could list the various psychotherapies; behavior modification; minor and major psychotropic medications, including estrogens and anti-androgens;

875

aversive conditioning techniques; electroshock therapy; physical castration; electronic brain stimulation; and lobotomy.) More importantly, as the *Kaimowitz* case implies (see Appendix), the most dramatic, irreversible, and high-risk intervention could become the *quid pro quo* for a sex offender's release from confinement.

The potential for abusing sex offenders by the use of less dramatic interventions certainly exists. A behavioral modification program (the START program) has been publicly discredited and dropped from the federal prison system,[29] while the use of apomorphine and succinylcholine to provide aversive stimulation as the "reward" for undesired behaviors has aroused such public outrage as to discredit those members of the correctional and psychiatric professions who condone their use.[30-31] Undeniably, it would seem, there is a need to monitor the use of certain treatment modalities with sex offenders, not only to protect such "patients" but to prevent psychiatrists and their medical colleagues from willingly or unwittingly becoming agents of social control with punishment rather than treatment as their assigned function.

The doctrine of informed consent viewed theoretically

One method for monitoring certain treatments given to confined sex offenders would rely upon the doctrine of informed consent whereby the offender would have to agree to the treatment before it could be initiated. Under this doctrine, the sex offender would be allowed an effective right to refuse certain treatments by withholding consent initially or by withdrawing during treatment already begun. Given the degree to which society has denied sex offenders control over the circumstances of their confinement and rehabilitation, requiring informed consent prior to certain treatments may seem unacceptable if not preposterous. Upon closer examination, however, such a policy may offer significant merits.

Rather obviously, the sex offender would often welcome an opportunity to influence the circumstances of his rehabilitation by consenting to, or rejecting, certain treatments offered. He might, for example, withhold consent in order to avoid high-risk treatment, or he might take a calculated risk and consent to certain treatments as the price for early release. Either way, the sex offender assumes a significant degree of responsibility for his own treatment during confinement insofar as the doctrine of informed consent forces him to take an active rather than a passive role within the treatment process.

Advantages. There could be psychiatric advantages to such a policy as well, for the requirement of informed consent within the context of sex offender treatment tends to establish the more traditional psychiatrist-patient relationship. Ideally the sex offender-patient would be given the option to accept (or reject) certain treatments and even to participate in planning those interventions with his psychiatrist, while the "system" would be precluded from imposing treatment despite the wishes of these parties. The rapport and trust encouraged by applying the doctrine of informed consent in this manner would seemingly support psychotherapy and, to some extent, even somatic techniques succeed in part through placebo effects.

Disadvantages. There are, of course, certain disadvantages in allowing sex offenders to accept or reject the treatments offered them. Beyond the difficult decision of determining which treatments should and should not be governed by the sex offender's consent, there is the reality that informed consent is an ongoing process. Beyond the initial dialogue, informed consent is reaffirmed as the patient continues to participate in the treatment process. Moreover, the doctrine requires patients who, in addition to being legally competent, are capable of comprehending the information offered them about proposed treatments. Finally, the doctrine of informed consent assumes that the patient's decision will be voluntary and not coerced. In terms of its legal definition, then, the doctrine of informed consent as applied to the sex offender poses criteria that may be difficult to meet: (1) sufficient *knowledge* (information) about the contemplated treatment, (2) a *legally competent* patient capable of comprehending that information and communicating a decision, and (3) the absence of coercion sufficient for the patient's decision to be *voluntary*.

To define informed consent solely in terms of its legal elements (knowledge, competence, and voluntariness) may only alienate the clinician and obscure important aspects of its application to the treatment of confined sex offenders. In terms of its clinical applications, the doctrine might better be defined in terms of: (1) characteristics of the intervention under consideration, (2) characteristics of the patient (or subject), and (3) characteristics of the milieu in which the consent is being sought. Each of these characterisitics, in turn, is defined along a continuum which, at its "lower" end, would not require as strict adherence to the requirements of informed consent as it would at its "upper" end in order to protect the prospective patient or subject from harm.

Relevant characteristics of the intervention, for example, could include its potential risks and benefits to the patient *and* to society (and the availabilty of that information for communication); its social acceptance (perhaps as a matter of public policy); its uniqueness in terms of available and suitable alternative interventions; and its reversibility either if the intervention is discontinued or, if irreversible at that time, in terms of stepwise increments of irreversible effects as treatment progresses. Relevant characteristics for the patient include not only the ability to comprehend information but perhaps the capacity to seek additional information and to communicate decisions rationally. Finally, the milieu within which consent is obtained should allow a "voluntary" decision; within the context of the confined sex offender, however, this characteristic might better be defined in terms of those degrees of coercion or inducement that cannot be eliminated from the setting but that are nonetheless acceptable as a matter of public policy.[32]

Informed consent as an ongoing process

However defined, informed consent is not a static event within the context of providing treatment for sex offenders. It occurs instead as an ongoing process, subject to fluctuations throughout treatment. Many factors contribute to alterations of the consent over time: new knowledge about the risks and benefits of proposed treatment modalities, shifting competence of the individual offender to assimilate new information, and subtle, but important, environmental influences, which reflect, to a greater or lesser extent, coercion relevant to the consent process.

Conceivably one would not require a sex offender's consent for treatments seen to present low risks and both high and immediate benefits for the patient and for society (with good availability and communication of that information), plus a high degree of social acceptance, easy reversibility, and little availability of alternative treatments. This would particularly be the case for persons of unquestioned competency who could comprehend the information and reach their decision in an environment that did not offer unacceptable inducements for consenting to (or unreasonable punishments for refusing) the offered treatment. Conversely, those interventions that might be defined at the other extremes of the continua would require a more stringently defined in-

formed consent for their initiation or might even be prohib-
ited altogether as a matter of public policy. The mechanism
by which such value judgments may be made will become
clearer as we focus upon certain currently available treatment modalities and their definition in terms of the criteria
noted in Table 1.

TABLE 1
Characteristics of Interventions and Sex Offenders Warranting
Differential Applications of Informed Consent

Least Stringent Controls ←————————→ Most Stringent Controls

INTERVENTION CHARACTERISTICS

1. *Degree of potential risk:*

Risk to patient is low; risk to society is low.	Risk to patient is high; risk to society is high.

2. *Extent of potential benefit*

To patient is great and immediate; to society is great and immediate.	To patient is slight or nonexistent; to society is slight or nonexistent.

3. *Availability of risk/benefit data:*

Procedures and results of intervention are well established.	Unavailable—procedures and results of intervention are largely or wholly unknown.

4. *Reversibility of change:*

Totally reversible at any time; or, if irreversible, occurring in "dose-related" fashion.	Totally irreversible at any time; or poor result if reversible after initiation of the intervention.

5. *Social Acceptance:*

Socially traditional; medically and socially ethical; economical, expedient, of demonstrable utility.	Socially radical, innovative; medically and socially unethical; costly, inefficient, of dubious utility.

6. *Availability of alternatives*

Intervention necessary, and no other alternative modality available.	Intervention necessary, but more suitable modalities available.

COMPETENCY OF OFFENDER

Able to comprehend relevant information	Totally unable to comprehend relevant information.

VOLUNTARINESS OF CONSENT REQUIRED

Initial patient consent without unreasonable inducement; freedom to withdraw during intervention without bias.	Initial patient consent coerced; no freedom to withdraw; or freedom to withdraw only with severe penalty.

7

TRADITIONAL PSYCHOTHERAPIES

What can be said about traditional psychotherapy with respect to the treatment of sex offenders? Two immediate problems arise when this question is posed: Who is being treated and for what specific purpose? The need for accurate psychiatric assessment cannot be emphasized too strongly in view of the socio-legal mixture that comprises sex offender groups. Further, all of the usual precautions in making any generalizations about the effectiveness of psychotherapy are in order. Encompassed under this grouping are not only types of individual and group therapies but subtypes of individual therapy, which vary from psychoanalysis to supportive or abreactive types. The usual uncertainties in the use of these treatments operate with respect to sex offenders and sexual behavior even if the sole criterion is simply a goal of changing behavior, ignoring other goals such as self realization, resolution of unconscious conflict, having a satisfactory therapeutic encounter, confession, or simply feeling better.

Certainly, the wide variation of individuals in the role of therapists, with a parallel variation in their training backgrounds, must be considered as one of the crucial independent variables in the effectiveness, or lack of it, of these treatments. It is not our purpose here to add another review about the results of psychotherapy. Enough research already exists to indicate the high degree of uncertainty with respect to therapeutic outcomes for all therapies. Some variety of psychotherapy is still probably the most prevalent form of treatment used with sex offenders. The quality of its delivery is what varies quite widely. Therefore, some of the general features that operate when these treatments are employed with sex offenders are presented.

The model used for discussion of the various types of treatments applicable or tried with sex offenders will involve five main points: (1) risk, (2) benefit, (3) reversibility, (4) medical/social acceptance of procedures, and (5) voluntariness of consent.

Risk

Psychotherapies are conceptualized as being on the minimal end of the risk scale. This is true when they are compared to various types of chemical or surgical treatments available and also in comparison to some of the aversive conditioning techniques. Yet, because of the complex subtleties that emerge in the therapeutic relationship, which are often ignored in pedestrian considerations of treatment carried on in coercive settings, risk is not absent. The type of risk is not as apparent as physical damage or irreparable injury sustained in the course of organic therapies. Rather, it appears in the context of transference-countertransference reactions. The types and manifestations of the unconscious go far beyond the realm of an overt expression of sexual deviance. Hence, the dangers that arise are in the nature of complex human emotions in the therapist and the patient which neither participant may understand or be capable of handling.

One of the inherent difficulties present in the psychological reaction of individuals who have committed a sex offense or who are committed as irresponsible about their sexual activities is the degree of denial present. In most cases the offender is not someone who is complaining about his own behavior. He may be upset about some of its consequences, but the behavior is sufficiently rewarding so that it is perpetuated or resorted to when he is under stress. In the private setting, when wives or lovers become sufficiently upset about some of the sexual practices in their mates, resort may be to treatment in a clinical setting. In the public setting, once legal visibility has occurred, the people most unhappy with the behavior are either the victims who feel exploited or law enforcement officials whose duty it is to maintain the peace and harmony of a community.

Dovetailing with the defensive denial in the offender is the type of denial witnessed in the general public as well. Public denial is in the service of not directly perceiving the meaning of the act in terms of an attack as well as sexual aggressiveness. Denial seen in therapists manifests itself by their not emphasizing the limits of their therapeutic capacity or by promising more than they can deliver. In essence, the main risks lie in the area of false expectations by all concerned. For the patient, a surplus of extra distortion lies in the disillusionment and rage that subsequently arise. Nor can the risk be separated from the unclarified assumption that if a person subjects himself to a particular treatment regimen, he will improve and society will subsequently change its attitude toward him. Since there has often not been an acceptance within himself that something really does need changing with respect to his sexual proclivities, the potential for rage remains.

Benefit

Given these types of risks, what possible therapeutic benefits can be offered in their place? The answer is evident if the general theory holds that the product of effective treatment is relief from psychological neurosis (and despair from such conflict). Of course, this general statement is the goal sought with *successful* treatment, and the benefits remain in terms of probabilities. This should hold true for any of the treatments—psychological or organic. Since the factors cited about individual variation in treaters, treatment settings, and techniques all vary, even apart from differences in individual patients, it is difficult to make more than a summary statement about what the benefits are from a psychotherapeutic approach for any given individual.

The hope is that the patient will be able to confront and deal with the nature of the conflicts that have led him to engage in whatever sexual misconduct has caused personal and social trouble. Accomplishing this goal requires sufficient ego strength in a person to deal with this kind of material. It also requires sufficient motivation to do so. If motivation cannot develop over time, the chances for benefiting from a psychotherapeutic approach are minimized. As part of a psychotherapeutic approach there must be a meeting of minds between the therapist and patient on the outcome goals selected. If the therapist is working toward the resolution of previously unconscious conflicts while the patient is working toward the earliest possible release from an onerous situation (e.g., his confinement in a security hospital or probation), the goals do not coalesce.

Attention is called to the need to educate the patient initially in terms he can understand as to what the therapy in question involves. Education of the patient is important not only for therapeutic purposes but to prevent later adverse consequences. If the goal of the therapist is to work through pathologic defenses, the existence of quite different goals in the patient militates against a common purpose. The usual errors are that goals are kept too general, remain too narrow, or lack specificity. For example, goals of enhancing the self-concept of the sex-offender or promoting his marital harmony may very well be part of the overall hopes of therapy, yet they are so generalized that they do not convey how these benefits will be achieved in the course of treatment. An example at the other extreme is therapy in which the goal of eliminating sexual activity with children is announced, with the therapeutic process directed solely at that activity without taking cognizance of the need to deal with additional personality factors. An entire discussion of the varieties of psychotherapy would be needed for further clarification.

Unfortunately, the field of therapy continues to be split by differences as to what the treatment processes and goals should be. Although the philosophies behind the various therapeutic modalities—psychoanalytic types of therapies, brief therapies, group therapies, and behavior modification—overlap to some degree, there is bound to be some difference in their points of view.

Little agreement exists on what should constitute the specific gains and objectives of treatment programs.[33] As a result, little agreement exists on the criteria by which to judge and evaluate their effectiveness in terms of what is feasible to accomplish. Some objectives are possible with certain techniques and others not. In this sense, the need for an accurate diagnostic assessment again becomes clear so that the therapist is aware of personality antecedents to aid in selecting meaningful therapeutic goals. A male who compulsively attacks anonymous women sexually will need treatment techniques and goals that differ from those of an adult male who exposes himself to children. The viewpoint taken of personality development and functioning bears a relationship to how one will view later dysfunctioning and conflict, particularly with respect to sexual conduct that violates the law or threatens to do so. In turn, the viewpoint on personality development determines what one thinks should be carried out as treatment. It is not our purpose to advocate one particular psychotherapeutic approach over another *per se*. Rather, we simply wish to advocate conceptual clarity in the setting of goals. If that is accomplished, all parties concerned will have an opportunity for commitment to the therapy most likely to be successful in terms of the goals selected—or not to choose any therapy.

Reversibility

One advantage of the psychotherapies is the comparatively minimal problems in the area of reversibility. They are minimal to the extent that we are not talking about tissue alterations or the possible unknown effects of changing chemistries or hormones within a person under treatment. However, by the very seeking of change, if psychotherapy is successful, the main forces guiding an individual's behavior in certain ways will, hopefully, have been vitiated. As an example, if treatment of the conflicted aspects involved in a compulsive rapist is successful, and the person later seeks to resume this type of behavior in response to stress, rape might no longer be available to him. Dealing successfully with the affects and defenses giving rise to these behaviors means that the need to behave in such a manner has supposedly been altered. The degree of reversibility into the old self would likewise be vitiated. Even in nonorganic therapies reversibility is not complete.

Medical/social acceptance

The problems associated with medical/social acceptance for various types of psychotherapy involve many of the issues implicit in what types of therapy would seem most indicated for the particular conflicts and ego strength of a given person. While other constraints relevant to acceptance operate (e.g., time, finances, and quality of personnel), a fundamental assessment deals with the individual tolerance for what is being proposed. In critical terms, medical/social acceptance basically deals with a delineation of the indications and contraindications for a particular type of therapeutic intervention. There is probably a higher degree of acceptance by the medical community and society for traditional forms of psychotherapies than for most of the other treatments discussed in this report.

Voluntariness of consent

Voluntary consent for commitment to a psychotherapeutic engagement raises different questions from those concerned with submitting oneself to organic therapies. Submitting to organic psychiatric treatments is closer to traditional medical procedures, such as surgery, in which something is done to one's body. Perhaps the basic distinction is that one cannot simply go through the format of treatment and mark time when an organic therapy is used. It can be imposed within limits once steps for informed consent are met legally, even in a sex offender who has no real belief in its efficacy. Stereotactic surgical procedures, for example, need not be carried out on a willing patient who is ardently seeking such a treatment.

In the psychotherapy scheme one may go through treatment as a form of game playing, such as showing up for appointments and even making verbal utterances, in the absence of the type and degree of commitment required for a meaningful therapeutic relationship. Game playing does not establish that psychotherapy is being accomplished. All types of problems arise when such attempts at treatment are carried out in the coercive setting of a security hospital, such as that used for most sex offenders or potential sex offenders. Perhaps one of the greatest hoaxes perpetrated on jailers and the jailed, as well as treaters and the treated, is the hoax that a process of treatment is actually being carried out simply by observing the formalities. "Perhaps it is impossible for the treatment setting to function for persons who are indefinitely condemned to treatment they do not want or from which they cannot benefit."[34]

At least a time restriction on psychotherapy makes it possible to limit the extent to which voluntary consent is given. A time limit can be used to offset the possibility that therapy is only a ritual. Unless some type of mutual collaboration can develop over time, and a goal be agreed upon, the question of whether or not treatment is actually being effected under the guise of continued custodial situations always looms. The significant variable in this treatment model is not just that of a verbal assent by a patient that therapy can take place. Rather, it is the added evaluation by the treater that he is willing to treat and that over time such treatment can actually transpire as evaluated mutually by the two parties and perhaps a neutral third party. Where such evaluations do take place, serious questions need to be raised about the nature of the patient's cooperation. The degree to which consent is voluntary, and to which treatment is meaningful to a patient, are the ultimate tests.

8

BEHAVIOR MODIFICATION

While there are many varieties of behavior modification techniques, it is the manner of their application that is questionable. Simple token economies may be coercive and deprive persons of constitutional rights,[35] depending on how they are employed. The point is that coercion may take place in any therapy. Aversive therapies, which vary according to the strength of the aversive stimulus (e.g., emetics, shock, drugs), can pose considerable risk. However, not all behavior modification methods need entail such risk. Assertiveness training or systematic desensitization are examples of a lesser degree of risk. It is grossly unfair to indict, as some have done, all behavior modification approaches as being potentially very dangerous and very risky.

Many learning theory approaches have been employed in the treatment of sexual deviation. Studies attempting to alter sexual behaviors by way of different behavior modification techniques have been conducted and reviewed.[36] There is such a variety of techniques classified as "behavior modification" that confusion is promoted. Lists include classical aversive conditioning with drugs, shock, instrumental escape and avoidance conditioning with shock as the aversive stimulus, aversion-relief techniques, positive training, systematic desensitization, and aversive imagery techniques, to name a few. Behavior modification as a generic type of treatment model need not involve only aversive techniques. For example, desensitization techniques are reported in the treatment of unwanted homosexuality or behavior shaping techniques in the treatment of exhibitionism. All behavior modification techniques cannot be categorized as ineffective when considering the evidence for their efficacy, nor can the potential risk or dangers to patients resulting from application of these techniques all be viewed as comparable. Some behavior therapy approaches are gaining acceptance among different mental health groups, which are not restricted to psychologists.[37]

Question of sufficient evidence

The significant question is whether the evidence is present that a particular behavior modification approach is efficacious for a particular type of sex offense, or, more specifically, a particular type of sexual psychopathology. Evidence for the validity of behavior modification approaches is often presented in the literature in the form of case reports that note changes in the frequencies of sex behaviors from a pretreatment to a post-treatment state (e.g., aversive shock for pedophilic behavior or shame aversion for exhibitionism).

Well controlled, large series of cases do present evidence for change in homosexual behavior, in part as a result of aversive methods.[38-39] When compared to failure rates for traditional therapies, the results of behavior modification techniques in terms of changing homosexual behavior look impressive. Nevertheless, most workers using only aversive methods have a hard core of 30-40 percent of patients who fail.[40] Some failures emerge as individuals who have previously had no reinforcing heterosexual experience and consequently have no behavior to replace that which they wish to extinguish. A history of pleasurable heterosexual encounters occurring prior to therapy and the absence of severe personality disorders of the narcissistic or impulse-ridden type are good prognostic signs in this type of therapy but also in any other type. Hence, these are significant variables in evaluating any treatment approach used with sex offenders because the absence of certain personality limitations will improve cure rates. The potential importance of increasing the patient's heterosexual responsiveness and providing social retraining, assertive therapy, or other means to complement the use of any aversive techniques is now being realized. Some investigators stress that aversion therapy must be viewed as any other treatment and, therefore, can only properly be undertaken within the full context of psychiatric management with attention paid not only to eliminating deviant behavior but also to eliminating the potential repercussions in the patient and his relatives. For example, a change in deviant behavior may affect the dynamics of a marriage, which may then require psychiatric attention itself.[41] Once these broader foci and consequences of treatment begin to be considered, the treatment model shifts focus away from strict change of one behavior, such as homosexual activity.

It is also important to remember that the behavior modification research that has involved sex deviation has tended to focus on homosexual behavior. However, this is often not the central concern of sex offender legislation and its applications, which are more concerned with violence or involvement of minors. Few investigative studies using behavior modification have involved persons charged with the more serious offenses of rape, aggravated rape, sexual assaults, and the multitude of sexual behaviors coercing children. Perhaps this is because it is easier to do research with subjects who are more readily available. Minor offenders (e.g., exhibitionists, voyeurs, transvestites, or persons charged with nonaggressive acts involving children) also pose less troubling questions about dangerousness. Again we are back to a position of observing that treatment of sex offenders and reports of results often involve groups that cause society the least concern.

Considerable difficulties exist in extrapolating from

studies using aversive shock procedures in the modification of homosexuality to their appropriateness and potential effectiveness for the management or treatment of institutionalized sex offenders. The motivation of the patient is a key variable in treatment, yet it may be neglected when conclusions based on motivated outpatients are applied to committed offenders. Patients whose motivation for treatment rests solely upon external coercion, such as legal proceedings or family pressures, are ignored for treatment in many treatment settings. It would be desirable in studies to stress the importance of concomitant involvement of other family members and opportunities for the patient that help to open up more satisfying or alternative means of functioning. For example, in emphasizing the efficacy of aversive shock for homosexuality, the opportunity to establish object relationships with a woman is stressed as the treatment goal. Even under ideal outpatient circumstances, comprehensive psychotherapeutic approaches have not demonstrated a high percentage of lasting behavioral change. In one study only two of eight patients persisted in changed behavior two and one-half years post-conditioning.[42] It is unclear whether the meager success rates reported in the literature over the long run are the result of poor techniques, ineffective therapists, or adverse environmental factors. These same factors militate against any successful therapeutic endeavors. In addition, there is always the problem of psychopathological conditions that do not respond to treatment. The lack of success is especially apparent when the technique is used within coercive institutional settings since there is little or no opportunity for the offender to develop alternate means of functioning. On the other hand, to carry out treatment outside of a hospital setting raises the issue of community safety.

9

PROBLEMS UTILIZING AVERSIVE TECHNIQUES

The discussion will employ the five main approaches discussed previously: risk, benefit, reversibility of procedure, medical/social acceptance, and voluntariness of consent.

Risk

Risk to the patient must be differentiated from risk to society. The risk to the patient of various aversive treatment modalities would include some degree of unpleasantness or painfulness as an inherent part of the proceedings. Reference is made to the necessity for fairly high shock intensity.[43] Others argue that the punishing stimulus should be as intense as possible.[44] Although aversive methods need not necessarily be acutely painful, a clear danger for their abuse exists. In one experiment succinylcholine was used to induce hypoxia and apnea in a behavior modification program for sex offenders in a prison hospital at Vacaville, California. The dosage level was sufficient so that anxiety was experienced in terms of fear of death by the subject.[45] Although objectively the risk may not have been on this level, the experiment was terminated since it was seen as too abusive and litigation was threatened. The risks may outweigh the benefits even without an actual fatality threat. On a more subtle level, the clinical risk of such treatment may be the persistence of apprehension and anxiety for long periods, which will vary from subject to subject. Post-treatment effects need consideration as part of the risk.

895

However, in numerous studies employing mild electrical
shocks as the aversive stimulus there is a lack of clinical
evidence that conditioned fear or anxiety develops in the
post-treatment response. In general, indifference, rather
than fear and anxiety, is a more common response to the
deviant stimulus after aversion therapy.[46] In the absence of
retraining, however, this indifference could be considered a
"risk" if diminished enjoyment of sexual activities became a
generalized result.

Risk to patients. Evaluation of the degree of risk in patients
is partly a function of one's vantage point. How the patient
perceives his situation, and the theoretical stance of the investigator, are only two variables. Aversive treatment involves four major areas of possible risk: (1) physical danger,
(2) emotional harm, (3) in effectiveness, and (4) "dehumanization" (for both patient subjects and perhaps experiment-
ers).[47] There are also potential risks for other behavior
therapies. "Flooding techniques" and consequent inability of
the subject to escape the deviant stimulus might induce emotional distress, but premature termination of aversive stimulation may reinforce the deviant behavior.

Token economies. Mention should be made of "token
economies." Routine ward management of patients often
employs these techniques without labeling them. Such
therapies are "coercively" administered in the sense that the
patient-subject is not given the choice of whether or not to
participate—again a question of consent (an example is the
discontinued START program used by the Federal Bureau
of Prisons).[48] Token economies may not be useful in the
treatment of sexual disorders *per se*, but they are useful as
components of more general retraining programs. The risks
here are the ill effects upon a confined subject of a situation
constantly involving potential loss of the amenities, and even
the necessities, of everyday life, such as restriction to quarters
in an already closed institution, withdrawal of outdoors

privileges in a routine already marked by lack of exercise, or loss of certain foods from an already unappealing or unhealthy diet.

Risks to society. Assessment of societal risks raises questions of value and social policy. A practical issue with respect to all of these treatments is their likelihood of failure in the sense of recidivism balanced against behavioral change. There is an implicit suggestion that "dangerous" and unmodified sexual offenders will be released erroneously as "cured." From the societal perspective the risk is that aversive behavior modification techniques give one man authority to do to another legitimately and legally what is questionable ethically. The threat is that society may stand to benefit more than the individual, which is more in keeping with penal practices.

However, there is also the significant question of what to do after the treatment is completed since there is no guarantee of protection from future dangerousness. The choice becomes one of which behavioral control (prison or aversive shock) is more controlling or less "dehumanizing." In making such a choice, decision-makers and the public need to discriminate clearly between expressions of optimistic intent and actual therapeutic practices. There is societal danger in rationalizing or legitimizing sadistic behavior whether under a cloak of punitive treatment or even "humanism." Few can deny that punitive measures have been carried out under the guise of "treatment." This is a particular hazard with respect to patient groups based on sexual deviance who arouse intense negative emotions such as anger, rage, shame, disgust, or scorn in the general public and possibly in some therapists.

Benefit

For the patient the benefit of aversive techniques presumably lies in the future decrease of offending behaviors if the

treatment is effective. Confusion results when the benefit to
society of eliminating objectionable sexual behavior is greater
than the actual benefit to the individual. The most acceptable
model is that in which treatment is sought voluntarily either
as a means of promoting behavioral change to reduce future
legal contacts or alternatively when the offender is discontent
because of the personal discomfort consequent to his deviant
sexual behavior. The patient is motivated because his present
behavior is either ego-dystonic or dysfunctional, and he desires to change. States of sadness or loneliness in some offenders may be alleviated by treatment. Under some treatment
situations the main benefit to an offender might be his release from an institution as part of a contract, if he agrees to
try treatment, on the condition that he will then not be
further institutionalized.

   Benefit analysis in the treatment of sex offenders is complex. From an authoritarian or "treater knows best" posture
one could always argue that treatment for these "abnormalities" restores normal functioning. In time, this perspective incorporates the view that a certain treatment is prefera-
ble for the offender even if he does not recognize it. This
parens patriae notion can be subject to wide abuse. It is also
necessary to consider change in behaviors versus change in
feeling states, self-esteem, mood, self-image, and so on. In
one of the frequently cited studies establishing the value of
aversive shock treatments in homosexuality, homosexual behavior was altered. However, the patients did not improve
(compared to a control group) with respect to symptoms such
as depression, isolation/loneliness, and feelings of inferior-
ity.[49]

   The criterion to evaluate benefit to society ultimately rests
on the elimination or reduction of subsequent offending
behaviors. Costs of treatment, rapidity of treatment, need for
specialized treatment personnel and procedures, and neces-

sity for institutional versus outpatient settings all require consideration. With respect to the "effectiveness" issue, the various behavioral modification treatments, including the least objectionable of the aversive techniques, can be considered to have limited value as treatment modalities. Their claimed effectiveness is for a restricted behavior. If the treatment is successful, it may prove valuable for those who are placed on probation for outpatient treatment. For the more dangerous behaviors, which sex psychopath statutes primarily focused upon, the treatment results of aversive conditioning techniques remain debatable.

Reversibility

Behavioral treatments frequently include "booster" sessions since induced changes may decay over time. Changes in clinical condition, with few exceptions, are both reversible and stepwise in progression. Theoretically, the patient's symptomatic sexual behavior could be retrained or conditioned to its original state. However, a more problematic issue involves the lasting or traumatic effects on the personality associated with the type of treatment received or consequent to effects of the treatment setting itself.

Medical/social acceptance

Acceptance of aversive treatments for sexual offenses has been challenged by both professional and other groups. The fear of "brainwashing" or using treatments for political or social control is always a threat. Increasing publicity about the use of various behavioral conditioning techniques for diverse purposes by governments sensitizes the public to potential misuse. Public suspicion appears to be balanced against a growing professional acceptance based on estimates of current effectiveness. Professionals must keep in mind the potential for abuse of this treatment modality.

Voluntariness of consent

The use of aversive behavioral modification techniques with sex offenders raises questions regarding the degree to which consent for such treatments can be considered truly voluntary in nature. Given the inherently coercive nature of institutional settings for sex offenders, submitting to treatment may be perceived as (essentially) the only route available for early release from confinement. Such submission can hardly be viewed as voluntary, especially when the risks of such treatments would otherwise be seen to outweigh their potential advantages. Alternatively, submitting to experimental treatment programs involving aversive conditioning may seem desirable (even without any impact upon eventual release) if such participation carries with it a special status within the institutional walls in terms of other inmates or the administration. The loss of special privileges or freedoms might significantly affect the voluntariness of consent for aversive conditioning procedures.

Conceivably, the voluntariness of consent might change during the course of aversive conditioning procedures. Consent, once freely given, may seem an unwise choice during the unpleasantness of punishment, but it may then be more difficult to withdraw from further participation in light of peer or therapist pressures to continue.

Finally, voluntariness of consent may depend rather critically upon the amount of valid risk/benefit information offered potential sex offender participants or upon their ability to comprehend such data. Insufficient and/or misleading information, as well as an inability to assimilate data, may taint the consent process, making it essentially involuntary.

Insofar as the best consent possible for aversive conditioning treatments involving confined sex offenders remains somewhat involuntary in nature, it is necessary to affirm, as a matter of public policy, the degree to which such treatment options should be offered to sex offenders at all.

10

ORGANIC TREATMENTS

In addition to the diverse types of psychotherapeutic and behavioral modification procedures, a variety of organic interventions have been receiving increased discussion for the treatment of sexual offenders. These procedures include (1) castration, (2) psychotropic drugs, (3) hormonal preparations, and (4) psychosurgery. The same conceptual approach employed for the other treatments will be used here without any pretense of rendering an exhaustive survey of the relevant clinical and experimental literature. Rather, the focus is a critique of what these treatments can now offer the sex offender. It should also be acknowledged that the risk-benefit ratio may change as further knowledge is accumulated.

Castration

Risk-benefit. Castration is a removal of the testes. The goal is to decrease hormone production with a hoped-for concomitant lowering of the sexual drive and a resultant lessening of criminal, sexually assaultive tendencies. Although surgical castration is an extreme measure ("the total treatment") and one which may now be superseded by other approaches, it continues to have strong advocates. Those who do not currently support this method stress new, safer, and less risky approaches.

As with many treatments for sexual offenders, the few

investigations of any systematic sort have come from Europe. More than 15 years ago follow-up studies on legally authorized castrations were performed in Denmark, Germany, Holland, Norway, and Switzerland.[50] The findings were that the consequences of surgery were minimal outside of the sexual sphere. Few adverse consequences were noted in other areas of physical functioning. The same study also refers to an interesting follow-up done with 215 castrated Norwegian men which indicated the possibility that 13 percent experienced deteriorating health or death. The actual results remain elusive. The effects of castration upon nonsexual criminal activity appear to be negligible. Castration appears to be a desperate measure consented to "voluntarily" by those who feel hopeless about controlling their sexual impulses in an open society where such behavior is not tolerated and otherwise leads to incarceration.

The European study cited reported recidivism rates in the general range of two to three percent, although in a follow-up of psychotics remaining institutionalized, eight to ten percent engaged in sexual acts that would have led to arrest had they not already been confined. One cannot ignore the conclusion that even when under institutional surveillance, a sizable number of psychotic sexual offenders persist in their deviant behavior despite the radical treatment measure employed.

Figures on recidivism are as difficult to appraise with castration as with all of the other treatments used with sex offenders. If recidivism is used in isolation as the only measure for the success of a treatment, it would be invalid. Sturup reported on the medical screening and evaluation of applicants for castration among the inmates at Herstedvester Detention Center in Denmark, a facility housing those who have special tendencies to commit repetitive sex crimes or who have committed other serious crimes.[51] He believes that castration is the answer when no other practical measure is available which appears safe both for the patient and for society.

Adverse effects, beyond variable treatment results, are difficult to pinpoint from the limited number of patients for whom adequate evaluation is available. Questions are always prominent about how intensely an investigator is looking for adverse consequences. Post-castration depression or suicide, precipitation or intensification of existing neurotic or psychotic equilibrium, and continued general aggressiveness have been noted.[52-53]

There is also the problem of a persistent sexual drive in some patients with the accompanying frustration and distress that may be handled in nonsexualized ways, criminal or otherwise. In some, frustration may become manifest as increased aggressiveness in the form of physical assaults or in increased irritability. Some castrated sex offenders also react with anxiety to their genital defectiveness and mutilation. Removing part of their external genitalia can accentuate other difficulties. Unfortunately, this type of multivariable evaluation is exactly what is needed most and what is omitted in longitudinal studies concerning the effects of castration as a treatment for sex offenders.

Reversibility. Reversibility is an obvious deficit in castration since the testes, once surgically removed, cannot be reinserted, although plastic prostheses may be inserted for cosmetic and/or psychological reasons. Nor is fertility regainable in the absence of the testicles. However, administration of testosterone can restore erective potential, although such treatment again increases the risk of restoring the motivation and capacity for criminal sexual behavior as well. What needs emphasis is the questionable efficacy of such an operation on complex acts that have multiple forms of expression, such as sexually assaultive or coercive behaviors.

Medical/social acceptance. The acceptance of castration for sexual offenders in the United States is quite low among both

professionals and the general public. Perhaps the threatening overtones of what could be done under the name of
treatment for deviance raises too many apprehensions about
adopting this solution. Eliminating reproductive capacity
raises anxiety even when done to limit family size.

The difficulty in gaining acceptance for this procedure
can be illustrated by the case of two 45-year-old men who
had spent two years at California's Atascadero State Mental
Hospital after pleading guilty to sex offenses involving minors.[54] After two years, hospital officials reported that the
men had failed to respond to psychotherapy (which types
of psychotherapy performed by whom were not specified) and
that they remained "dangerous to society" with little or no
prospect of improvement. Upon being returned to a county
jail to await an indeterminate sentence, the two men re-
quested castration (giving waivers to their lawyers, the judge,
and the court-approved surgeon to perform a bilateral or-
chidectomy) in hopes of obtaining probation as part of a
rehabilitation program. After consulting with 50 fellow
urologists, the San Diego County Urological Society and the
Malpractice and Ethics Committee of the San Diego Medical
Society, the surgeon withdrew his agreement to do the
surgery. Medical society officials informed him that, despite
malpractice insurance, he might be liable to a lawsuit for
mayhem or assault and battery regardless of waivers. These
types of issues make acceptance by society and the medical
community of castration as a suitable treatment for sex offenders subject to continuing debate.

Voluntariness of consent. This, too, is debatable. How voluntary can a consent be when given by an inmate faced with a
long-term prison sentence or an indeterminate civil commitment? The voluntary nature of such conduct is open to
serious question. Many complexities present in giving
consent may be operating between the inmate and the
authorities raising castration as an option. While some in-

dividuals may be acting in a self-punitive manner, some authorities may be seeking retribution under the cloak of surgery. Perhaps the crucial issue is by-passed when it is put in the context of consent not being possible for one who is involuntarily detained. Rather, the question should be whether it is desirable on legal, medical, and social grounds to prohibit an individual in such a predicament from seeking this means to change his behavior and/or gain release from many years of institutionalization. Yet, this question must be balanced by the overtones of such procedures whereby freedom is obtained by castration.[55]

Psychotropic Drugs

Risk-benefit. It may seem unnecessary to comment on the use of psychotropic drugs as a mode of treatment for sexual psychopaths. Yet, this group of individuals, as with the remainder of the general population, whether in or out of an institution, is frequently receiving psychotropic medications. The risks involve the possibilities of adverse side effects from drugs that are not curative, in any sense of the word, for the types of disturbances that lead the sexual psychopath into legal difficulties. Nor are they useful in the sense of removing any specific symptomatic sexual aberration. (We are excluding those few individuals whose sexually offensive behavior was associated with a psychotic mental illness. In such a case the question becomes the usual clinical one of selecting the most appropriate psychotropic drug for the diagnosis in question.)

The benefits of psychotropic medications for sex offenders supposedly operate indirectly by way of altering anxiety or mood states. The inference is that in a secondary manner the drugs act to reduce the propensity to act in a criminal sexual manner. Such an inference is precarious if there is a reliance on these medications alone as the primary treatment for sexual psychopaths. The use of these drugs as an adjunct to make the person more comfortable must be balanced against adverse side effects and misguided optimism. In most cases resort to psychotropic drugs as a treatment for sex psychopaths may be a result of inadequate diagnostic appraisal, or misunderstanding, of the specific types of psychopathology present in these individuals.

Reversibility. Reversibility is governed by the nature and severity of adverse side effects associated with the different psychotropic medications. If we are talking about reverting to a previous emotional state, such as becoming more anxious again when taken off a tranquilizer, we are simply noting whether the drug has been effective regarding a certain affective state such as anxiety.

Medical-social acceptance. Acceptance of psychotropic medications by the medical community and the general public appears quite high. There is no need to emphasize the wide prevalence of their use in the United States as indicative of such general acceptance. The problem may be too easy an acceptance by resorting to the prescription pad when the indications are minimal.

Voluntariness of consent. Psychotropic medications may be sought by institutionalized inmates as a means of easing their burden of confinement. The nature of possible side effects and the limitations of this mode of treatment for the problems that led to their institutionalization need to be stressed as part of their use. It is a different situation if these drugs are administered parenterally against an individual's wishes, which raises questions about the justifications for such treatment without an inmate's consent.

Hormonal preparations

The hormonal drugs usually recommended as treatment for sex offenders are specifically antiandrogenic in nature. However, of the many individuals with sexual problems, most are given some type of tranquilizer and/or antidepressant medication, as is the rest of the general population whether in or out of an institution. While these types of medications may alter anxiety or mood states and thereby supposedly alter the propensity to commit a sex offense, this is a precarious inference to make if we are to rely on these medications alone as the primary treatment for those against whom sex statutes are directed. Hence, the additional resort to estrogens and antiandrogens to effect a "functional castration."

Risk-benefit. Hormone preparations offered the hope that antagonizing the male hormone, androgen, would lessen sexual urges. Again, the next step in the reasoning may be articulated: Acts of sexual violence will be lowered once the hormone balance is altered. Different types of estrogen compounds are used, such as estradiol B.P.C. implanted subcutaneously or estradiol valerianate given as an intramuscular depot. Stilbestrol given orally or parenterally in continuous or intermittent form is also used to obtain similar results.

One of the primary benefits to the sex offender and society is the ease of administering this form of treatment. Troubling side effects (e.g., gynecomastia, fluid retention, headaches, nausea, and possible thrombophlebitis or aggravation of seizures) make questionable any reliance on the offender to self administer the medication. Failure to take medication by the antisocial individual raises especially difficult problems, particularly when his sexual behavior has become an integral part of his psychopathy. Perhaps some innovative method to guarantee a timed dosage release by surgical implantation is part of the technological solution. If the medication succeeds in reducing sex drive, and concomitantly criminal behavior, the benefits to the individual and society of permitting him to live in the society are great. Again, the problem becomes apparent in terms of the relative ease of achieving control over an individual when he is institutionalized compared to maintaining control while free in a community.

The current impetus is to supplant estrogens with antiandrogen drugs. These seem to cause fewer side effects and, thus, are more acceptable to patients. In Europe cyproterone and cyproterone acetate have been used experimentally although not in the United States.[56] Depo-Provera (medroxyprogesterone acetate), a synthetic steroid, lowers plasma testosterone levels and may be used in an effort to reduce potency and ejaculation. This is presumably accomplished by shutting off the testicular production of the male sex hormone although the drug may function directly on the central nervous system as well. Reportedly, there is a loss of drive or a lessening of tension and anxiety. Apathy about sexual activity gains prominence, however, as potency of sexual desires wanes.[57] Many of the proposed benefits remain uncertain due to incomplete research that has not resolved certain methodologic inadequacies or established these drugs as a cure for criminal sexual behavior.

Reversibility. Reversibility is available with estrogens in terms of altering effects upon libido. Reversal occurs within a few weeks following cessation of the drug, but the sex drive then returns. An early study reported degenerative changes in testicular biopsy material secondary to oral stilbestrol.[58] While impotence is reversible, there might be adverse consequences in a marital relationship if other outlets are chosen and found gratifying in place of a regular sexual life. Again, we must rely on clinical reports in the absence of systematic research investigation that considers many aspects of an individual's life. With Depo-Provera there are no known permanent adverse side effects, and apparently potency and ejaculation are reversible when treatment stops, although the number of research subjects reported upon at this time is small.[59]

Medical/social acceptance. Acceptance of hormone treatment by the medical profession appears to vary widely. Given the relative ease and safety of administering hormonal treatment to an individual who has perpetrated repetitive sexual acts on unwilling partners, social acceptance is more readily available. The antiandrogens are currently in a state of experimentation, and their medical acceptance should be viewed in that context. Untoward side effects, with accompanying publicity, will lower the acceptance level.

Voluntariness of consent. Consent carries with it the same restrictions that operate in other treatments at a time when the recipients are incapacitated in institutions and facing long-term stays when consent is obtained. For the antiandrogen drugs, consent must be given with cognizance of the experimental nature of the treatment. With both hormonal approaches, if there is freedom to withdraw from the drug, a period of up to a month exists until drug effects disappear. There is no immediate reversibility. Enforced injections, of course, are contrary to any type of voluntary consent.

Psychosurgical Approaches

Among the many topics challenging mankind, the mind-body problem, or the relationship between the brain and behavior, is always of interest. Witness the science fiction accounts of brain control seeming to portend where technology will go (e.g., brain stimulation, site implantations with added remote controls, and procedures of increasing sophistication to ablate parts of the brain). *Psychosurgery,* or "functional neurosurgery," means selective ablation or destruction of brain tissue, or the cutting of certain interconnecting neuronal pathways in the brain, with the stated purpose of altering thoughts, moods, emotional reactions, or social reaction patterns. The goal is to alter, and hence to control, certain aspects of behavior. The surgery is carried out in the absence of established structural disease or damage to the brain in contrast to surgery for well established anatomic diseases. Thus, temporal lobe resection to control the manifestations of temporal lobe epilepsy, or resection of a tumor, are not within the formal definition of psychosurgery. They are rather part of *neurosurgical* procedures undertaken in the presence of diagnosed anatomic abnormalities. The assumption that sex offenders must have damaged tissue or altered physiology and that psychosurgery will repair this deficit even though an anatomic deformity or malfunction cannot be demonstrated is treacherous. It opens up an untenable scientific position. If a position is taken that psychosurgery should be used, whether or not altered brain tissue or function is ever demonstrated, we are relying on a hypothesis that cannot be falsified. It leaves us with no provable way to reject the hypothesis since those advocating psychosurgery assume that their surgical procedure applied to a legal category (sex offenders) will be remediable for the sexual behavior.

In the past few years, considerable research attention has been focused specifically on the use of psychosurgery for the modification of violent or aggressive behavior by placing lesions in areas of the brain believed to be involved in such behavior.

In the past three decades, attention has turned from the radical prefrontal lobotomy to procedures and techniques with much more refined precision effecting alteration or ablation of small areas of the brain. These stereotactically placed lesions of a few milliliters in volume may be made in the limbic system and elsewhere. The most frequent sites of such intervention are the cingulate gyrus, the amygdala, thalamus, and hypothalamus. In addition, many other techniques to alter brain tissue are currently available: injecting alcohol, freezing, suction, diathermy, beaming ultrasonic beams or gamma and beta rays through the skull, and implanting radium and yttrium seeds.[60]

When it comes to applying these psychosurgical techniques

to sexual disturbances, they extend from control of aggression and violence to control of sexual behavior, which may or may not be fused with aggression. This complicates evaluation of results. Only one group has actually made zealous claims in this regard.[61] There are four major reasons why the outcome from these procedures is difficult to evaluate: (1) Diversity of symptoms is present in any patient population selected for psychosurgery. With sex offenders, this raises the problem of using psychosurgery and claiming results for treating "aggressive rapists," for example. However, "aggressive rapists" do not constitute a clinical grouping; they are rather a heterogeneous group of offenders. There is also the assumption that similar manipulations carried out on the brain will control diverse types of sexual aggressions. (2) Preoperative evaluation and information are often lacking, especially with regard to clinical indications that psychiatrists deem most relevant. A quote from several decades ago still seems apropos: "No surgeon wishes to be a technician only. In most instances, however, the neurosurgeon does not have the proper training nor has he the time to devote the many weeks and perhaps months of intimate contact with the patient and his relatives to reach a just decision. Therefore, he is not in a position to weigh justly the merits for or against operative interference."[62] (3) The usual follow-up problems are present: lack of detail concerning the degree, character, and thoroughness of postoperative evaluations with respect to behavioral and psychosocial variables. (4) Ambiguities are left unclarified as to what types of past treatments have been performed, to what degree, and at what level of competence. Many factors are relevant, such as past drug treatments (which drug, dosage, duration), past psychotherapy (what type, by whom, changes in the course of treatment), and types of institutional settings (what kind, what was done, reaction of inmate).

Risk. Risks go far beyond those simply attendant on routine surgical procedures. The brain, as an organ, is still considered more sacrosanct than most other organs of the body and not simply from superstition. This is partly due to its being the seat of intellectual functioning and the higher learning processes characteristic of man. There is also the prospect of the basic altering of the "self" when the brain is surgically altered. Although it is hoped that psychosurgery will be beneficial, the degree of unpredictability is great. As noted, the scientific rationale for psychosurgical intervention is quite tenuous. Experimental procedures may have been performed on lower forms of animals, but the generalizations and logical inferences drawn therefrom are questionable. A pervasive problem is that there are no agreed upon diseases or conditions for which psychosurgery is the treatment of choice. In fact, some advocate psychosurgery for very mild emotional disturbances.[63] An eminent neurosurgeon concluded that the evidence at hand indicates that those mental patients who do not respond to "protracted intensive medical management should be appraised as possible candidates for [psycho] surgery."[64] Balanced against this more extreme position is one where specific indications of organic brain disease must be present (e.g., the signs and symptoms of a seizure disorder) with aggressive sexual manifestations as an accompaniment.

The distinction between neurosurgery to correct diagnosed organic conditions (e.g., epilepsy or intractable pain) and psychosurgery as an experimental procedure to alter symptoms or behavior, or carried out as a result of a certain legal status, needs continuing emphasis. Some argue that it is not brain malfunction but rather behavioral manifestations that are, in fact, being treated by amygdalotomy.[65] Since many behavioral problems are amalgams of the biopsychosocial, critics fear that psychosurgery opens the possibility for controlling deviance of many shades which can change at different historical periods. Nor is the argument persua-

sive that the logistics from the small number of neurosur-
geons in the United States (about 3,000) make the threat
unrealistic. The threat is that the procedure could be performed selectively on dissident groups or their leaders.

Some of the side effects of psychosurgery have been emotional blunting or a decrease in spontaneity. General retardation does not appear to occur, but specific types of deterioration have been reported in the past such as impairment in
abstract thinking, lowered ambition and motivation, defec-
tive planning and foresight, and impaired conscience. Some
of the effects might control criminal sexual acts, while others
might accentuate the behavior by lowering controls and in-
sight. Again, the lack of precise and adequate follow-up, due
to the lack of sensitive indicators, plagues attempts to appraise the consequences of these procedures in different
dimensions. Appraisal will become more important as a result of the variety of psychosurgical procedures that have
now developed.

Benefit. Analysis requires appraisal of just what the alleged
benefits are. Presumably, a societal benefit of simply making
recalcitrant and dangerous patients less of a custodial burden
for hospital staffs no longer suffices as a justification for
psychosurgery. Often the justification is circular, pointing
out that psychosurgery "works" and, therefore, what else is
needed? Is it an isolated symptom, such as a tendency to
assault young boys, that is being changed? Or is it rather
some generalized goal that is sought such as lowering the
level of aggressiveness? Related to this is how we assess the
validity of alleged personality change if an individual is then
to be released from an institution. If broader criteria are
used, such as social adjustment, all the pitfalls associated with
multiple variable analysis emerge. Some reports claim fantas-
tic improvements (up to 94 percent) after cingulate surgery
for affective illness.[66] Again, if these benefits are actual,
appraisal of specific symptom change and psychosocial ad-

justment needs documentation. The possible benefits—to relieve an individual of his predilection to carry out criminal sexual activities and thereby avoid continued institutional detention—are too great to avoid if the positive evidence is persuasive. At present we can only say that psychosurgical intervention is an experimental procedure. It needs much more specific confirmation, along with connection to specific psychiatric syndromes rather than legal categories.

In the realm of psychiatric treatment, history tends to repeat itself endlessly, as any review of new or altered treatment programs reveals. Criticism on multiple bases of almost all of the psychosurgical reports is possible. Early claims for success often change. For example, initial reports of success in altering rage reactions via psychosurgery gave rise to a two million dollar lawsuit against the same physicians four years later for turning the patient into a vegetable.[67]

Reversibility. Reversibility is eliminated since these are anatomic lesions. Yet, interestingly, there is the problem of symptom recurrence, so that outcome results may not actually be irreversible. Cingulotomy studies have shown an immediate postoperative improvement in some patients, but over time, many experience a progressive return of symptoms. This again raises the question of what might be revealed by a thorough follow-up of these procedures.

Medical/social acceptance. Acceptance is questionable. While physicians and the public can accept neurosurgical treatment for certain refractory organic conditions, psychosurgery raises many unknowns. It is acknowledged that there are some persons of different disciplines and persuasions who advocate these procedures, particularly since they find the organic model of illness appealing. The majority of physicians and lay persons, however, would not appear to find the procedures acceptable. Psychosurgical intervention for sex offenders is seen as having a very high risk/benefit ratio since its purpose is to control unacceptable behavior as much as to treat an individual. Acceptability thereby is diminished.

Voluntariness of consent. Issues of consent are quite relevant to any type of surgical procedure. This is especially true if the patient is institutionalized since consent to psychosurgery may be overtly or covertly suggested as a means of gaining release. Such a forced choice raises a question about the voluntariness of the decision reached. Furthermore, problems exist of the competency of the subject to assimilate material and exercise his judgment in a psychological sense about such complex procedures. There may be difficulty in obtaining any genuinely voluntary consent under these circumstances. Whether these options should even be available in institutional settings that are inherently coercive or whether consent can be sufficiently voluntary in such environments are matters of public policy. Psychosurgery should not be performed upon children, prisoners, mentally retarded persons, or involuntarily committed mental patients. (See Appendix for a discussion of the *Kaimowitz* case, which raised many issues about the nature of consent in these patients.)

11

GUARANTEEING ADEQUATE TREATMENT

The history of all groups handled through civil commitment procedures is weighed toward a legal emphasis on *procedural* due process in contrast to *substantive* due process. What happens to these individuals once removed from society has been, until recently, relatively ignored. For those civilly committed as mentally ill, judicial scrutiny has been increasingly extended to an area originally thought to have little need for it. The assumption in hospitalizing those diagnosed as ill was that, in placing sick people involuntarily in hospitals, the state was acting benignly in the best interests of its citizens. Similar overtones were present in sex psychopath legislation with their format of hospitals, a civil commitment process, and treatment for those whose sexual conduct made them appear dangerous.

Over time the supposedly benevolent intervention of the state based on the theory of *parens patriae* was seen to conflict with other individual rights, such as autonomy and freedom. The state could also intervene simultaneously through its police power to protect the health, safety, and general welfare of its citizens against "dangerous people." Specifically, those committing crimes involving sex, or behaving in an unacceptable manner sexually, were seen as needing compulsory treatment—to protect the community if not themselves. Treatment of sexual psychopaths would then be to maintain safety for the remaining citizenry.

919

Procedural due process

It may seem paradoxical in a report advocating repeal of sex psychopath statutes to introduce material related to guaranteeing adequate treatment. We do not see it as paradoxical since a realistic viewpoint does not, unfortunately, see these statutes disappearing for some time. Hence, it is justifiable to argue in favor of confined individuals' receiving the best remedial measures available which presumably have something to do with why they have been committed. Individualization in the setting of treatment goals for those confined by sex psychopath statutes, with the means, for implementation made available, permits something more than warehousing. We believe a key initial element in setting the stage for effective treatment requires that a committed person feel his legal rights were protected in process. Eager acceptance is not necessary. It is rather a realization that there has been a maximum protection of a right not to be so committed against one's wishes before such a legal commitment takes place. In this context procedural due process rights take on an initial significance regarding the respect afforded an individual not to remove him from society without stringent rules in the process. Once this barrier has been passed substantive due process rights enter with respect to what treatment will be provided once he is committed to a security hospital.

A summary of questions relevant to procedural due process for sexual psychopathy will illustrate some of the difficulties. Variations in statutory requirements for commitment of this group have been discussed earlier. Attention was called to the fact that some statutes permit commitment of sexual psychopaths without either a conviction of a sex crime or even a charge being brought; in these situations there is no bar to prosecution at a later time. Half of the statutes do not provide for a jury to determine whether someone is a sexual psychopath.[68] Variations in the quality of the examiners and the examinations have been noted. The defendant may not be allowed to introduce his own expert medical witnesses in some states. At the commitment hearing, cross-examination of witnesses may not be permitted.

In a federal case in Wisconsin, twice remanded on appeal, civilly committed mental patients were extended constitutional protections available to criminal defendants.[69] These were: (1) the right to counsel at an early stage of the proceedings, (2) a prompt preliminary hearing, (3) a speedy final hearing, and (4) a standard of proof for their commitment identical to that used in criminal trials. Perhaps these are forerunners of rights that will be sought under sex psychopath statutes. The indeterminate nature of most sex psychopath statutes always raises the possibility of a longer period of confinement than a prison sentence for the same behavior.

Equally important are the variable standards for release which seem vague and subjective. Attempts may be made to keep a person confined in prison after serving a maximum sentence on a sex charge by having him committed as a sexual psychopath. In one case this was invalidated on grounds that no treatment was being provided at the prison.[70] What would have satisfied the court, if treatment was being provided at the institution, raises concern about the possibility of such continued detention if perfunctory treatment efforts are present. The Supreme Court has held that a person who has served a maximum criminal sentence in a prison cannot continue to be held on the alleged basis that he is mentally ill and dangerous. A separate hearing for a civil commitment is required at the time the prison sentence expires to establish that he is currently mentally ill and dangerous.[71]

One procedural due process right that is shifting is the "standard of proof" required for commitment as a sexual psychopath. The customary standard prevailing in routine civil commitments has been based on "preponderance of the evidence" (about a 51 percent likelihood). The shift is toward the standard of criminal proceedings of "proof beyond a reasonable doubt" (about a 90 percent likelihood).[72] Related is the "burden of proof" standard where the state assumes the burden of proving that the defendant meets the increased standard for commitment as a sexual psychopath, or conversely, the defendant rebuts the assumption and shows that it has not been demonstrated beyond a reasonable doubt that he is a sexual psychopath in need of special commitment.

Recent cases involving sex psychopath commitments indicate the following trends: (1) Miranda-type warnings may be required that the examinations by clinicians are not privileged communication and, hence, may bring about commitment as a sex psychopath;[73] (2) periodic judicial review of the need for continued institutionalization will be required;[74] (3) it will become increasingly difficult for sexual psychopaths to be confined in units maintained in penal institutions, or mingled with the general penal population, and not have this interpreted as cruel and unusual punishment in violation of state and federal constitutions;[75] (4) insertion of police reports into trial records will be ruled on as unacceptable hearsay and not covered by the hearsay exception to expert testimony; (5) sex psychopath statutes may be held to be in violation of the due process clause of the Constitution as witnessed by cases in Pennsylvania and Alabama.[76-77]

Appellate activity relating to the constitutionality of sex psychopath statutes has relied heavily on the United States Supreme Court's decision in *Specht v. Patterson*.[78] The court there indicated that it agreed with a Colorado Court in a sex psychopath commitment that constitutionally decided:

Petitioner therefore was entitled to a full judicial hearing before the magnified sentence was imposed. At such a hearing, the requirement of due process cannot be satisfied by partial or niggardly protection. A defendant in such a proceeding is entitled to the full panoply of the relevant protections which due process guarantees in state criminal proceedings. He must be guaranteed all those safeguards which are fundamental rights and essential to a fair trial. . . .[79]

Substantive due process

As long as any individual is detained by way of sex psychopath statutes, a responsibility exists to provide treatment. It is not enough to point out that a person may be dangerous; many dangerous people are released from prisons every day. Presumably, something more is required in terms of substance when someone is committed as a sexual psychopath. Increased scrutiny is demanded to insure that "something more" beyond incarceration is provided.

The institutionalized sexual psychopath has many legal rights: adequate habilitation, protection against deterioration or harm while institutionalized, compensation for work (antipeonage), humane living conditions, education, marriage, the right to vote, and the right to the "least restrictive alternative" if confinement is seen as necessary. While legal cases delineate which of these rights are enforceable, and in what settings, these rights are really no more than what people claim is their due, despite their institutionalized status. One of the damaging byproducts of withholding any rights is the sense of injustice experienced. Sex offenders may have pre-existing problems related to a sense of injustice, so that when the promise inherent in the nature of commitment is ignored, the problem is compounded. Legal strictures established concerning the special handling of juveniles are equally applicable to sexual psychopaths in that "unbridled discretion," however benevolently motivated, is frequently demonstrated to be a poor substitute for principle and procedure.[80]

No need exists to demonstrate the problems that arise when concepts are borrowed from separate disciplines and applied toward different goals than those intended. A preliminary question exists: Does a sexual psychopath need any special treatment? In California the sex psychopath statute includes a finding "as to whether or not the person would benefit by care and treatment?"[81] This is a shift from establishing a need for treatment *per se* to predicting whether the outcome of treatment is likely to be beneficial for a given person. A similar result occurred in Wisconsin in response to a case where it was held that a sexual psychopath could not automatically be committed for treatment upon conviction without a special hearing.[82] A recommendation for "special treatment" as a sexual psychopath utilized three criteria: (1) Was the offense the product of sexual psychopathology? (This actually infuses criteria of criminal responsibility.) (2) Is the individual "potentially responsive to available specialized treatment assuming adequate motivation"? (3) Is the individual "sexually dangerous"? A person is recommended for specialized treatment as a sexual psychopath if criteria (1) and either (2) and/or (3) are present. More recently the United States Supreme Court held that a retardate could not be held as incompetent for trial indefinitely without the confinement bearing some relationship to the purpose of the confinement, namely treatment for restoration of competence.[83] This holding has special implications for situations in which sexual psychopaths with poor prognoses are being retained in institutions, and only perfunctory efforts are being made to provide treatment. A further anomaly exists when the treatment offered has little bearing on the sexual behavior that led to the commitment. For example, treatment measures such as remedial education or vocational training are not more than tangentially related to the type of sexual psychopathology that led to community concern and commitment.

Few can be satisfied with approaches that entail little more than incapacitating a sexual psychopath by locking him up in a hospital. Such practices, closer to a policy of preventive detention, are not in keeping with manifest legislative intent or judicial inquiry.[84] Nor are they consistent with the therapeutic purposes of a hospital in contradistinction to a prison. In one case a sexual psychopathic patient was transferred from a mental hospital to a prison on the rationale that this was part of his treatment in helping him learn self-discipline.[85] A court ruling held this unconstitutional since a man who had not been tried or convicted by a jury could not be confined in a penal institution. The patient was ordered returned to the mental hospital for treatment. However, no question was raised by the court about what conceivably would be provided in the hospital that had originally transferred the patient to a prison.

Nor can confinement under a sex psychopath statute be for "remedial" purposes only and then be carried out among the "hopeless and violently insane."[86] Because such individuals have never been found legally insane, their detention on a ward with regressed and combative patients violates the remedial spirit of the statute. In the California statutory scheme, mentally disordered sex offenders were committed to "institutional units" in prison among the general penal population and without treatment. This was seen as constituting cruel and unusual punishment in violation of the State and Federal Constitutions.[87]

In the District of Columbia the absence of adequate treatment led to *habeas corpus* proceedings to seek release. This approach has been used with individuals detained as mentally ill by civil commitments as well as those confined by criminal commitments. A man detained as a sexual

psychopath claimed treatment was not available at St.
Elizabeths Hospital in the District of Columbia. Mopping
floors and watching television for years were not judicially
accepted as treatment. The man had been committed as a
sexual psychopath after exposing himself, a misdemeanor
punishable by 90 days imprisonment if convicted. The
United States Circuit Court explicitly stated, "Indefinite
commitment under the sexual psychopath law is justifiable
only upon a theory of therapeutic treatment."[88]

Guaranteeing treatment

An enormous volume of professional and lay literature is
presently appearing dealing with means of guaranteeing
treatment. Correspondingly, an increase in court challenges
has occurred to clarify what treatments are being administered, by whom, and whether treatments are correlated with
any particular efficacy. Confinement in a hospital as a sexual
psychopath may lead to no more therapy than a criminal
receives in a prison.[89] The future is one in which professionals working in hospitals will find themselves defendants in
suits brought by patients trying to establish justification for
their detention in the absence of adequate treatment.[90]

The pursuit of adequate resources to provide treatment
led professional groups, including the American Psychiatric
Association, to join in a suit against St. Elizabeths Hospital.
The atmosphere becomes heated when psychiatrists find
themselves defendants in a suit supported by their own professional organization. On the other hand, some urge a con-
servative use of scarce professional and financial resources.
Allocation of resources to security institutions might divert
time, money, and manpower from assessment and treatment
that could be given to individuals in communities. In stark
contrast to a choice between adequate resources for hospital
or community treatment emphasis is a humanitarian ideal

that holds society responsible for providing whatever is needed for institutional treatment (e.g., optimal patient-staff ratios, highly trained specialists, and an atmosphere that is therapeutic rather than punitive). Although these factors alone do not suffice to establish treatment, without them treatment cannot even be assumed to be occurring with any degree of certitude. If a committed sexual psychopath wishes to claim and exercise his right to receive treatment, and he can supposedly benefit from it, the "hardware" must be available.

A democratic government needs to articulate its goals clearly when it seeks to exact a price in terms of individual liberty. It is a cogent question whether or not indeterminate civil commitment for sexual psychopaths, with treatment minimal or absent, in a semiprison setting can ever be rationalized as treatment. If it is so claimed, continued detention *de facto* rests on what is ultimately a preventive detention basis—to protect a community from dangerous people. In the absence of treatment, continued detention in a security hospital begs the question of dangerousness without the opportunity to negate it. Such detention brings home forcefully the point that continued detention is not done for the patient's welfare but rather almost exclusively for the protection of society. However, to accept such a basis for detention of sexual psychopaths under special statutes seriously jeopardizes a position that loss of liberty and treatment are not casual things but rather deal with fundamental issues about how we dispose of some of our handicapped citizens.

In the absence of treatment, a hospital may be seen as tranformed into a penitentiary. Rouse was confined in a mental hospital after being found not guilty by reason of insanity.[91] His claim of a right to treatment was based on an interpretation of a statute that Congress had enacted as the civil commitment statute for the District of Columbia. Humane concerns were present since Rouse was confined three years after being committed for carrying a dangerous weapon (an act for which he would have received a year in prison). Sexual psychopaths are in similar straits, since the overtones of dangerousness which are so pervasive in their situation lead to continued confinement.

Constitutional considerations

Constitutional issues have been directly raised in several right-to-treatment cases. The "cruel and unusual punishment" aspects of the Eighth Amendment form one line of attack. The state may confine an individual to protect the general health and welfare of a community. However, if an individual is quarantined under such provisions, the stated purpose is for treatment so that he may be released as cured at the earliest possible moment. Isolating a patient with smallpox or tuberculosis is done not only for the public's protection but also for the treatment and ultimate release of the individual. To do otherwise amounts to cruel and unusual treatment.

A second line of constitutional attack involves either the "due process" or "equal protection" provisions of the Fourteenth Amendment. In fact, this was one of the major attacks mounted unsuccessfully on the constitutionality of the first sex psychopath statutes. At that time, the inherent vagueness of statutory provisions defining a sexual psychopath and the lack of criteria defining those needing "special treatment" were unsuccessfully attacked. Lengthy periods of detention can and do result when the vague definitions employed in sex psychopath statutes are applied to diverse types of sexual behavior.

The constitutional issues in right to treatment cases for those committed under sex psychopath statutes obviously touch many areas of clinical concern. Ambiguity as to the purpose of the laws leaves clinicians in dilemmas about their professional roles. People perceived as dangerous are not necessarily the most treatable. Discrepancies exist between the practical world of confinement for safety and the optimal world of the application of treatments with a fair chance for success. In addition, some committed sexual psychopaths do not wish to receive treatment at all.

Questions about the legal remedies available for convicted sex offenders who are warehoused in hospitals under conditions not much different than those in correctional facilities arise. Phrases such as "adequacy of treatment" themselves contribute to the ambiguity. At one end are those who view adequacy as implying no more than meeting decent standards of bed and board; at the opposite end are those who believe that adequacy implies not only reliance on generally agreed upon modes of treatment, but also that the required treatment should be carried out by those qualified and experienced in administering the appropriate treatment needed for an individual. Between these poles a continuum of opinion exists about treatment adequacy.

From this discussion it would be difficult to defend any policy of detaining nondangerous sexual psychopaths without treatment. In view of the Supreme Court's decision in *O'Connor v. Donaldson*, it is impossible legally to confine a nondangerous mentally ill person without giving him some treatment, since this deprives him of his right to liberty.[92] The court did not bother to define what adequacy of treatment should be for the committed mentally ill, and we are left with the same uncertainties for committed sexual psychopaths.

Once past the hurdle of nondangerous sexual psychopaths, the question of treatment when dangerousness is alleged continues to loom with all of the issues discussed throughout this report. Future legal cases can be anticipated at the juncture where dangerousness is alleged while treatment is minimal and ineffective. One proposal would deter-

mine dangerousness by a special hearing where the procedures and protections of a criminal trial operate.[93] In this
context, detention and simple custodial care are carried out
subject to periodic review of the diagnosis, prognosis, treatability, and assessment of continued dangerous status.

Right to treatment precedent

Earlier cases have suggested a constitutional right to treatment.[94] A most significant case arose in Alabama dealing
with adequacy of treatment issues (*Wyatt v. Stickney*, changed
to *Wyatt v. Alderholt*, and now *Wyatt v. Handin*).[95] It was
decided along with a Georgia case, by the Fifth Circuit
Court.[96] Even though the Supreme Court's decision in
O'Connor takes precedence over these cases (the Supreme
Court vacated the judgment of the Fifth Circuit Court, which
had relied on it), the reasoning is important since additional
cases will assuredly arise.

Wyatt was originally filed in a federal court in Alabama as a
class action representing involuntarily committed mental patients at Bryce Hospital; later the case was enlarged to include mentally ill patients at Searcy Hospital and mentally
retarded residents at Partlow State School and Hospital. The
class of patients ultimately included approximately 5,000
patients of whom 1,500 to 1,600 were geriatric cases and not
seen as mentally ill and another 1,000 were mentally retarded. The court listed in great detail what adequate treatment would involve for these patients under the Fourteenth
Amendment. Accordingly, the Alabama Department of
Mental Health was enjoined from continuing the existing
inadequate medical and psychiatric care along with substan-
dard physical accommodations. The decision held that the
state had failed to "promulgate and implement a treatment
program satisfying minimum medical and constitutional
requisites."

The appraisal of treatment standards given by the court in *Wyatt* offers a model with which to appraise and compare the treatment offered committed sexual psychopaths even though the case involved other classes of committed patients. Guarantees of treatment embraced specifics in three broad areas: (1) a humane psychological and physical environment; (2) qualified staff in sufficient numbers; and (3) individualized treatment plans. A humane environment included: (a) privacy; (b) a right to manage one's own affairs (including retention of driver's licenses, marrying, voting, and making contracts unless some specific indication of incompetence was present); (c) a right not to be subjected to unusual or potentially hazardous treatments (including lobotomy, ECT, reinforcement conditioning) without express informed consent; (d) a right to reimbursement under minimum wage laws for labor performed in the hospital unless done voluntarily; and (e) a right to physical accommodations of no more than six patients to a multi-patient room, one toilet per eight patients, adequate heating and air conditioning, and thermostatically controlled hot water.

On examining these standards it is apparent that they are not standards for guaranteeing treatment but rather minimum standards of decency below which a human environment should not fall. Only when these basics are met can the task of treatment programming begin. Licensing and certification requirements for those treating, comparable to those engaging in private practice in the same professions, would be required. This is significant in view of reports that many physicians working in state mental hospitals (40 percent of those employed in New York State mental hospitals) are not even licensed to practice medicine.[97] Similarly, nonprofessional staff would be required to have training and to work under the direct supervision of qualified mental health professionals (e.g., a psychiatrist who has completed three years of residency, a psychologist with a doctoral degree, a social worker with a master's degree, or a registered nurse with a graduate degree in psychiatric nursing).

Individualized planning legally forbids treatment based on arbitrary ward assignments or categories of diagnosis. Staffing ratios of different mental health professionals per 250 patients are required. Nor can mass assignments of patients meet medical standards for treatment. A comprehensive physical and mental examination, required within two days of admission, covers the details of a good psychiatric history, and it is available as part of the patient's medical record on the ward for whatever purpose is required. Within five days an individualized treatment plan must be drawn up, which specifies details within the perspective of the "least restrictive" treatment conditions required. The plan encompasses the goals and criteria for release. Within 15 days the patient is reexamined to determine whether hospitalization is still needed, and whether the treatment plan is being implemented. A post-hospitalization plan is considered part of guaranteeing treatment adequacy, with a particular mental health professional held responsible for implementation. The plan is reviewed at least every 90 days, along with a new mental examination.

Wyatt applied to committed sexual psychopaths

The *Wyatt* opinion has direct applicability to committed sexual psychopaths. If the standards are applied to public institutions in which sexual psychopaths are housed, not more than a handful of establishments could meet the criteria. Perhaps the situation with sexual psychopaths is worse in all respects than with other civilly committed groups. Because of the deplorable conditions, coupled with the ambivalence connected with the old problem of sexual dangerousness, pressure mounts for trying almost any treatment measure. There is the desperate hope that something will permit these people to be released from the hospital without endangering the community. The consequence is a push toward experimental or risky measures. Contrary to civil commitments of the mentally ill, the ambivalance about release of sexual psychopaths prevents the type of community dumping of sexual psychopaths into the melange of aftercare facilities which exists with the mentally ill; they are forced to remain in security hospitals.

One of the most difficult problems is deciding how to enforce standards. For many years the most acceptable aspect of the sex psychopath statutes was that they were being ignored. "The only thing that saves these laws from the tyranny of bygone ages is that they are not being enforced."[98] However, the laws remain on the books, and people continue to be processed and detained under them. Development of some type of system to evaluate treatment adequacy and guarantee its continuance is a first step for these unfortunates. Some believe guarantees will come about via an expansion of generalized medical insurance coverage, private or public. Although new and different sets of problems will arise from such an approach, it is naive to suppose that simply providing psychiatric health insurance will remedy the multiple and serious deficits existing in the provision of treatment for criminal sexual psychopaths. Until the sex psychopath statutes are repealed, there is a continuing need to rely on litigation, with specifics of treatment adequacy being spelled out by expert psychiatric testimony. Litigation and testimony present a viable option to move toward better treatment for greater numbers of sexual psychopaths as an interim measure. Legislation to guarantee treatment for those who are selectively detained is an even more progressive step.

12

CONCLUSIONS

Recommendations follow, based on the content of this report, involving the relationship between the mental health professions and their involvement under the sex psychopath statutes.

(1) *First and foremost, sex psychopath and sexual offender statutes can best be described as approaches that have failed.* The discrepancy between the promises in sex statutes and performances have rarely been resolved. In part, this discrepancy is due to practical exigencies, such as chronic problems of staffing and funding. Other problems lie in the fears of communities about sexual behavior coupled with naiveté about what sexual legislation could accomplish.

(2) *The categorization process projected by sexual psychopath statutes lacks clinical validity.* The notion is naive and confusing that a hybrid amalgam of law and psychiatry can validly label a person a "sex psychopath" or "sex offender" and then treat him in a manner consistent with a guarantee of community safety. The mere assumption that such a heterogeneous legal classification could define treatability and make people amenable to treatment is not only fallacious; it is startling. It is analogous to approaches that would create special categories of "burglary offender" statutes or "white collar" offender statutes and then provide for special commitments, such as to "burglary psychopath hospitals." The invalidity of this approach remains in the eighth decade of this century as

it was in the third decade when sex psychopath statutes began to emerge. There are many discrete clinical problems involving sexual dysfunction or perversion which are capable of amelioration by selective treatment measures. These require individualized clinical assessment and treatment, which are not achieved by some generic mixing as sex offenders. Sex psychopathy is a questionable category from a legal standpoint and a meaningless grouping from a diagnostic and treatment standpoint.

(3) *The ambivalence of the public about sexual deviance and sex crimes has never been resolved.* Public ambivalence leads to simultaneous desires to punish and to help. An unfulfilled social promise in this regard pertains to the goal of abandoning the classical notion of punishment (which was to be tailored to the crime). In place of this notion, methods of treatment and rehabilitation were to be instituted and carried out by mental health professionals in hospitals. Treatment approaches denied the degree of ambivalence felt by many toward sexual deviation and the attendant anxiety that sex crimes elicited. A mixture of conscious and unconscious motives regarding sexual conflict in the general population, along with the need for repudiation of certain sexual fantasies, constituted yet other sources that permitted the continuance of lackadaisical performance under sex psychopath statutes. The paramount emphasis on community protection is still prominent. The cloak of therapeutic help by means of indeterminate stays is used to perpetuate what is a form of community reassurance. The bankruptcy of indeterminacy as a treatment policy has been exemplified by legal challenges demanding that the justification or purpose of confinement be given beyond simply warehousing or making pretenses of treatment for sexual offenders.

(4) *Constitutional questions are involved on many levels.* As psychiatrists, we will not recapitulate with further detail the myriad legal issues touched upon in the body of this report.

The constitutional implications for individuals caught up in one of the webs of sex psychopath statutes require careful scrutiny. Vaguely worded laws that utilize the language of social reform mixed with psychiatric jargon have done more harm than good. Questions about the continued constitutionality of the statutes under present interpretations, procedural rights at the commitment and release stages, substantive treatment rights once committed, and restrictions in various treatment approaches from the organic to the psychological are a few of the major areas we have touched upon which raise constitutional issues.

(5) *The proper role of the psychiatrist when dealing with sex offenders is first and foremost that of a clinician.* We view the role of the psychiatrist in dealing with alleged sexual psychopaths caught up in legal intricacies as no different from his role when participating in other areas of the legal system, i.e., to offer thorough and adequate evaluation of the mental functioning of individuals who are involved. This role includes making individualized appraisals based on the presence or absence of psychopathology geared toward specific and relevant clinical questions. When some type of explanation for behavior is possible, it should be given; if not, vague generalizations and baseless predictions are to be avoided. We distinguish this clinical role from whatever others the psychiatrist wishes to take as a professional consultant or advisor in advocating changes within the mental health and criminal justice systems for dealing with sexual offenders.

Generalizations about sex offenders not grounded in empirical data from the individual case often do nore harm to the individual and society than no statements at all. The probabilistic nature of statements should be pointed out when research studies are cited, and the nature of such studies should be made clear. Treatment recommendations should be connected to the overall evaluation and diagnosis. They should not be left hanging merely to comply with some statutory phraseology, such as a yes or no answer as to whether "special treatment is needed" or whether a person "meets the statutory requirements of a sex offender." Nor need the psychiatrist hesitate to say that there are questions he cannot answer despite being pushed to give such answers.

A variety of psychiatric disturbances can give rise to symptomatic expressions that may violate a sex law, even though most disturbed individuals exist without experiencing such behaviors. These disturbances encompass neurotic conflict, sexual perversion without psychosis, periodic psychotic acting out, organic brain syndromes, and mental retardation to name a few. If specific treatment needs are indicated, they should be pointed out.There are many situations a psychiatrist can clarify by his contributions. For example, (1) if a perverse act that results in a sex crime is an integral part of a schizophrenic psychosis, this relationship should be pointed out to the court along with the types of treatment recommendations applicable with such a diagnosis. (2) Acts of burglary that are facades for carrying out sexual activities in homes should be explained as part of a picture of sexual psychopathology rather than simply considered property offenses. (3) A youthful mental retardate engaging in pedophilic behavior is indicating a need for community intervention on many levels involving psychiatry and education, as well as the legal system.

Dilemmas arise when it is realized that treatment might not be attainable in many public institutions. In these circumstances one alternative is for the psychiatrist to make a recommendation for the type of treatment he believes is indicated and leave the problem of implementation to the courts, legislature, and general public. Another alternative is for the psychiatrist to make no recommendation at all if he feels the treatment will not be implemented. The latter position requires that the psychiatrist have up-to-date information about the various facilities in terms of their personnel and the programs to which sexual offenders are sent. Perhaps the worst thing a psychiatrist can do is tailor his opinions to whatever compromised versions of treatment are currently being offered, thus putting himself in the role of sanctioning treatments in which he does not believe. Better either to state what is needed or offer no opinion at all. However, seeing that an offender actually receives the treatment he requires is a judicial and legislative responsibility, as well as a duty of the general public. It is the ambivalence of these groups, along with the pretense of treatment, which perpetuates the existing situations.

(6) *Predictions about "sexual dangerousness" are unreliable.* *Socio-legal* questions regarding the dangerousness of sex offenders really pertain to what kinds of acts, behaviors, or crimes should be viewed as dangerous. More specifically, they express a public judgement that certain behaviors are threatening to the community and, therefore, will be classified as dangerous, a concept that permits legal control to be maintained over such individuals. The confusion attendant upon efforts to specify what constitutes dangerous behavior makes these attempts subject to debate. As an example, should a sex offender whose act is connected with a psychotic mental illness be seen as dangerous while the same act in the absence of a psychosis would not be so classified?

Clinical questions, in contrast, are different. They involve assessment of people with different types of psychopathology and diagnoses in order to determine whether prognoses can be made about the likelihood of certain acts occurring in the future. Subvariations occur (i.e., the probability of change if treatment is secured), but the focus is on individual psychopathology. Even here, once the acts are appraised clinically, the question is what degree of expression is required before they reach the level at which legal intervention will take place. Clinicians must state in a straightforward manner that their ability to predict future dangerousness is quite limited. Predictions about recidivism for certain criminal sexual acts are even more difficult because of the extremely low base rate for such events. In essence, not only is the categorization as a sexual psychopath invalid from a clinical perspective, but problems of deciding which individuals are "sexually dangerous" and which not are often a product of chance, caprice, and vagueness. Is the legal system, along with its mental health consultants, really capable of making such discriminations? We think not and hope that psychiatry will not participate in the questionable undertakings of predicting future dangerousness when the results are so consequential to a person.

(7) *Possibilities for carrying out certain treatment programs or research have always existed.* Sex psychopath legislation, which was supposed to facilitate treatment and research, has rarely done so. But proposals for treatment and research with safeguards for individuals in line with the suggestions in this report have been and still are possible. It is not a justification for sex psychopath statutes to argue that research is needed. It is needed and it should be carried out, but these are matters separate from sex statutes.

Although we clearly recommend the abolition of sex psychopath statutes, nothing in this report should be interpreted as a rejection of voluntary treatment for sex psychopaths, or any criminal offenders for that matter. Such programs should ideally be available for those who can (and do) profit from them, with ongoing research to establish their efficacy. Participation may be selective, but treatment programs should exist. What we reject in particular is stigmatization by way of special sex psychopath statutes with an indeterminate nature and with generalizations about treatment, when the main goal is really to remove these people from society.

(8) *Community pressure to "do something" poses special dangers.*

It becomes socially dangerous when pressures build up and high risk procedures of a questionable nature are employed. We have pointed out problems that arise when pressures to treat lead to experimental procedures that lack adequate safeguards and are performed on captive subjects. As noted, sex psychopath statutes originated in situations of community and legislative pressure. Along with adverse consequences to the individual, there is the handicap a society labors under in deceiving itself that something worthwhile and effective is being done. In the end, the integrity of everyone is compromised.

(9) *Courts need a variety of meaningful options.* Greater options permit judges to exercise more selectivity about disposition. Both the judiciary and the public must realize that sentencing need not be a mechanical process. Poorly managed treatment programs carried out in a randomized and haphazard manner need not exist. The promise of individualized justice is something that can be attained parallel to the promise of offering individualized treatment to someone who exercises a choice over his wish to participate. Within these restrictions, our society should never be in a position of denying a person treatment for a psychiatric illness, that has been associated with his criminal sexual behavior, when he wants to receive it. If community safety is the primary goal, it can be meted out as for any crime. However, if other goals are also accepted, they should be clearly acknowledged and the means for implementation provided (including experimental measures). Courts are then in a position of knowing options do exist. However, it is difficult to justify indeterminate detention for categories of sex crimes when some of the most serious criminal acts of a nonsexualized nature are generally not so handled.

(10) *Sex psychopath statutes should be repealed.* This is a beginning step toward justice. Further, the term "sex psychopaths," which is devoid of psychiatric meaning, should

cease being used. If the special help and treatment some sexual psychopaths want and need are to be provided, it will not be through the types of laws now in existence. When an experiment has failed, it is time to say so rather than continue an exercise in futility.

13

APPENDIX: THE KAIMOWITZ CASE[99]

In the summer of 1973, three judges of the Circuit Court for Wayne County (Michigan) were empanelled to determine whether physicians at the Lafayette Clinic could perform psychosurgery upon a criminally committed and legally competent patient from another Michigan state mental institution, having first obtained the patient's informed consent for that procedure. Earlier, Lafayette Clinic physicians had obtained state approval to conduct a controlled investigation in order to determine whether psychosurgery (in the form of amygdalectomy) could reduce the risk of violent behavior for certain "dangerous" patients committed under Michigan's sexual psychopath statutes.

In addition to a detailed neurological screening, the research protocol required that a patient/subject's consent for psychosurgery would be subject to review by a panel of three persons not directly related to the research itself (a Monsignor, a certified public accountant, and a law professor knowledgeable in psychiatry). Ultimately, one candidate who had obtained psychiatric and neurological approval for participation in the study offered his consent for the psychosurgery; that consent was then approved by two of the three committee members. (The law professor had interviewed the candidate and found his consent valid but had delayed in communicating this opinion to other committee members.) Before the proposed psychosurgery could occur, however, the local (Detroit, Michigan) press not only questioned the efficacy but also the ethics of the research. Subsequently, a group of distressed citizens including an attorney, Gabe Kaimowitz (for whom the case was initially named until the identity of the candidate was known), successfully gained legal standing to bring action against the state on behalf of the candidate and those of his class. Soon after this class action was filed, the candidate in question (one John Smith) was discharged from the state hospital, thus mooting his case in particular. Nevertheless, both the Lafayette Clinic and attorneys for the plaintiffs sought a declaratory judgment from the Wayne County Circuit Court to determine, from a judicial perspective, the propriety of conducting further psychosurgical research under the proposal of the Lafayette Clinic.*

The *Kaimowitz* opinion may be divided into three general areas: (1) considerations of the risks attendant to the proposed psychosurgery, (2) legal requirements for informed consent, and (3) constitutional issues potentially raised by the research in question.

The circuit court's evaluation of the proposed psychosurgery

In dicta, the circuit court found the recommended amygdalectomy highly experimental in its apparent departure from established medical treatment. Likewise, the court

---

* It is not true, as is commonly alleged, that John Smith would have had to undergo the proposed psychosurgery as the "price" of release from the state mental hospital. Smith had been informed by Dr. Yudashkin (then commissioner of mental health in Michigan) that he would be released from the institution whether or not he consented to the proposed psychosurgery (personal communication to B.H., Professor Ralph Slovenko, October 23, 1976). Thus, it is not surprising that the Circuit Court of Wayne County, Michigan, did not address directly the constitutional and/or statutory parameters of requiring persons to undergo experimental psychosurgical procedures as the *quid pro quo* for release from institutionalization.

found that the psychosurgery posed potentially high risk and low benefit for the subjects involved as indicated by prior (animal) experimentation. Ultimately the judges questioned whether the patient would experience any greater control over his presumably dangerous potential as a result of the psychosurgery.

The court views informed consent

The court's assessment of the risks posed by psychosurgery was only a prelude to its establishment of the legal elements of informed consent, to wit: (1) (legal) competency, (2) knowledge of the procedure proposed, and (3) voluntariness of consent.

The judges did not set a specific level of intelligence as the minimum for finding legal competency but instead focused critically upon certain factors that might diminish a person's awareness of his circumstances. Thus, the judges stressed the sequelae of "institutionalization" whereby the committed person's basic integrity and capacity for making independent decisions were impaired. Moreover, the court would not countenance any delegation of the authority to give consent to the guardians of institutionalized research subjects who were deemed incompetent.

The court views the element of "knowledge"

Having emphasized the inherent risks of psychosurgery and the all but fatal impact of institutionalization upon legal competency to give consent, the court then considered the inability of patients such as the plaintiff in *Kaimowitz* (John Smith) to fully comprehend the risks of psychosurgery given the present state of our knowledge of that procedure. The court, in this section of the opinion, was not so concerned with the candidate's ability to comprehend information but with the scarcity of relevant data by virtue of the experimental and preliminary nature of the psychosurgery itself.

946   Sex psychopath legislation

The court and the element of "coercion"

Finding that institutionalized patients such as the plaintiff rarely participate in meaningful decision-making about the conditions of their treatment and confinement, the circuit court judges further reasoned that institutionalization may actually impair patients' capacities to make rational decisions even when given the opportunity to do so, as, for example, when placed in a position to refuse or offer consent for psychosurgery. In addition to impairing one's basic ability to make rational decisions, institutionalization would, to the court at least, appear by its very existence to exert significant pressures for patients to "cooperate" by consenting to dangerous procedures. In a word, the court found the circumstances of institutionalization to be inherently coercive.

In all three areas—legal competency, knowledge of the procedure proposed, and voluntariness of the consent—the *Kaimowitz* court ruled against the defendants and all but precluded research of the type contemplated by the Lafayette Clinic. Additionally, the judges concluded their opinion with a tangential reference to constitutional issues that might be raised by psychosurgery research. Thus, the judges reasoned, if the first amendment protects the freedom to express ideas, it necessarily protects the freedom to generate ideas. If one assumes that psychosurgery in physiological effect alters or jeopardizes the generation (if not the expression) of ideas, it would thereby be unconstitutional. Moreover, psychosurgical procedures such as contemplated in *Kaimowitz* might raise additional constitutional issues of cruel and unusual punishment.

Reaction to the *Kaimowitz* decision

The Circuit Court for Wayne County, Michigan, ruled that plaintiffs of the *Kaimowitz* class are incapable of giving informed consent for psychosurgery undertaken in the hopes of alleviating future dangerous behavior because they are, by circumstances of their confinement or by virtue of our lack of present knowledge, legally incompetent, unknowledge-able, and insufficiently free from coercion to offer a volun-tary and informed consent to psychosurgery. Likewise, the court implied that serious constitutional questions might be raised by experimental procedures such as contemplated in *Kaimowitz* by the Lafayette Clinic.

There was, and still is, divided enthusiasm about the *Kaimowitz* decision. Some believe that the court, whose opin-ion has not been challenged, has successfully ended all psychosurgical research in the United States. Others, who believe that the decision sought such an objective, believe that it instead drove psychosurgery research "underground" so that few follow-up data or control studies will be available to evaluate its ultimate efficacies and disadvantages. It is still too early to rule whether such an effect has indeed occurred. Still others would allege that the holding has essentially not been appealed because its application is narrow and because the judges themselves seemed ambivalent as to their ruling.

Perhaps the truth of the matter lies in a middle ground. It cannot be denied that the judges struck down any possibility of a study such as that contemplated by the Lafayette Clinic, involving, as it must, a narrow class of persons who were not found legally qualified to offer informed consent. This is not to say that similar research could not be done upon other populations, perhaps with better theoretical and experimen-tal support. Even then, the judges would caution that consent should be subject to the closest possible scrutiny and that insurmountable constitutional issues might ultimately bar even that research. The social policy message of *Kaimowitz*, insofar as the handling of the sex psychopath, seems clear: One cannot assume that potentially high-risk and low-benefit treatment within an inherently coercive environment may be legally carried out solely on the basis of the "consent" of the patient. Depending upon the stringency of its interpretation and application, informed consent can be utilized to limit the initiation of such treatment or monitor a research effort over time.

14

REFERENCES

1. Group for the Advancement of Psychiatry. PSYCHIATRICALLY DEVIATED SEX OFFENDERS, GAP Report No. 9 (New York: GAP, February 1950) pp 1-11.
2. L. J. West. "Thoughts on Sex Law Reform," in CRIME, CRIMINOLOGY AND PUBLIC POLICY, R. Hood, ed. (New York: The Free Press, 1974) pp 469-487.
3. W. E. Nelson. Emerging Notions of Modern Criminal Law in the Revolutionary Era: An Historical Perspective, *New York University Law Review* 42 (1967) pp 450-482.
4. G. L. Haskins. LAW AND AUTHORITY IN EARLY MASSACHUSETTS (New York: Shoe String Press, 1960).
5. I. L. Reiss. THE FAMILY SYSTEM IN AMERICA (New York: Holt, Rinehart & Winston, 1971) p 407.
6. M. Zelnik and J. E. Kanter. SURVEY OF FEMALE ADOLESCENT SEXUAL BEHAVIOR CONDUCTED FOR THE COMMISSION ON POPULATION (Washington, D. C.: Government Printing Office, 1972).
7. MASSACHUSETTS GENERAL LAWS, Chapter 272, Section 34, 1975.
8. D. H. Flaherty. ESSAYS IN THE HISTORY OF EARLY AMERICAN LAW (Chapel Hill, North Carolina: University of North Carolina Press, 1969).
9. Nathaniel Hawthorne (1883). THE SCARLET LETTER (New York: Modern Library, 1950).
10. S. Brownmiller. AGAINST OUR WILL—MEN, WOMEN AND RAPE (New York: Simon and Schuster, 1975).
11. BRACTON ON THE LAWS AND CUSTOMS OF ENGLAND, S. E. Thorne, ed. (Cambridge: Belknap Press of Harvard, 1968) Vol. II.
12. F. Pollock and F. W. Maitland. THE HISTORY OF ENGLISH LAW (London: Cambridge University Press, 1968) Vol. II, p 491.
13. E. P. Powers. CRIME AND PUNISHMENT IN EARLY MASSACHUSETTS (Boston: Beacon Press, 1966).

14. *Huebner v. State*, 33 Wis 2d 505 (Wis., 1967).

15. S. J. Brackel and R. S. Rock. THE MENTALLY DISABLED AND THE LAW (Chicago: University of Chicago Press, 1971). Michigan, New York, and South Dakota are not included among the 28 states with special sex psychopath or sex offender legislation although they have been in the past. In a revised penal law, New York did not reenact a provision for indeterminate sentencing and discretionary hospitalization of certain types of habitual offenders. The South Dakota statute only permits post-sentencing transfer of child molester prisoners to state hospitals for examination and then possible hospitalization.

16. MINNESOTA STATUTES, Chapter 526.09, 1974.

17. *Minn. Ex. Rel. Pearson v. Probate Court*, 390 U. S. 270 (1940).

18. DISTRICT OF COLUMBIA CODE ANNOTATED, Section 22-35-3, 1967.

19. J. W. Mohr. "Evaluation of Treatment," in SEXUAL BEHAVIORS: SOCIAL, CLINICAL, AND LEGAL ASPECTS, H. L. P. Resnik and M. E. Wolfgang, eds. (Boston: Little, Brown & Co., 1972) Chapter 21, pp 413-428.

20. H. L. P. Resnik and M. E. Wolfgang. "New Directions in the Treatment of Sex Deviance," in SEXUAL BEHAVIORS: SOCIAL, CLINICAL, AND LEGAL ASPECTS, H. L. P. Resnik and M. E. Wolfgang, eds. (Boston: Little Brown & Co., 1972) Chapter 20, pp 397-412.

21. K. O. Christiansen, M. Elers-Nielsen, R. S. LeMaire, and G. K. Sturup. SCANDINAVIAN STUDIES IN CRIMINOLOGY (Oslo, Norway: Universitet Sforlaget, 1965).

22. Georg K. Sturup. Treatment of Sexual Offenders in Herstedvester Denmark: The Rapists, *Acta Psychiatrica Scandinavica Supplementum* 204, 44 (1968) 1-63.

23. K. G. Gray and J. W. Mohr, "Follow-up of Male Sexual Offenders," in SEXUAL BEHAVIOR AND THE LAW, Ralph Slovenko, ed. (Springfield, Illinois: Charles C Thomas, 1965) pp 742-756.

24. W. R. Morrow and D. B. Peterson. Follow-up of Discharged Psychiatric Offenders "Not Guilty By Reason of Insanity" and "Criminal Sexual Psychopaths," *The Journal of Criminal Law, Criminology and Police Science* 57 (1966) 31-34.

25. L. V. Frisbie. Studies on Sex Offending in California: 1954-1966, *California Mental Health Research Digest* 4 (1966) 135-141.

26. H. L. Kozol, R. J. Boucher, and R. F. Garofalo. The Diagnosis and Treatment of Dangerousness, *Crime and Delinquency* 18 (1972) pp 371-392.

27. J. J. Cocozza. Letter to the Editor, *Psychiatric News* 8 (August 15, 1972) 2.

28. T. P. Hacket. The Psychotherapy of Exhibitionists in a Court Clinic Setting, *Seminars in Psychiatry* 3 (1971) pp 297-306.
29. Federal Bureau of Prisons. "Behavior Modification Programs," in HEARINGS BEFORE THE SUBCOMMITTEE ON COURTS, CIVIL LIBERTIES, AND THE ADMINISTRATION OF JUSTICE OF THE COMMITTEE ON THE JUDICIARY, House of Representatives, 93rd Congress (Washington, D.C.: U. S. Government Printing Office, 1974) pp 1-73.
30. *Knecht v. Gillman*, 488 F.2d 1136 (1973). See also R. G. Spece. Conditioning and Other Technologies Used to "Treat?" "Rehabilitate?" "Demolish?" Prisoners and Mental Patients, *Southern California Law Review* 45 (1972) 616-684.
31. M. H. Shapiro. Legislating the Control of Behavior Control: Autonomy and the Coercive Use of Organic Therapies, *Southern California Law Review* 47 (1974) 237-356.
32. R. J. Bonnie and P. B. Hoffman. "Regulation of Human Experimentation: A Reappraisal of Informed Consent," in SMU SYMPOSIUM ON HUMAN EXPERIMENTATION (Dallas: SMU Press, 1975).
33. H. B. Urban and D. H. Ford. "Some Historical and Conceptual Perspectives on Psychotherapy and Behavior Change," in HANDBOOK OF PSYCHOTHERAPY AND BEHAVIOR CHANGE, A. E. Bergin and S. L. Garfield, eds. (New York: John Wiley & Sons, 1971).
34. J. Katz. The Right to Treatment—An Enchanting Legal Fiction, *The University of Chicago Law Review*, 36 (1969) 755-783.
35. D. B. Wexler. Token and Taboo: Behavior Modification, Token Economies, and the Law, *California Law Review* 61 (1973) 81-109.
36. A. J. Yates. "Sexual Disorders," in BEHAVIOR THERAPY (New York: John Wiley & Sons, Inc., 1970) Chapter 12, pp 223-245.
37. American Psychiatric Association. BEHAVIOR THERAPY IN PSYCHIATRY, Task Force Report No. 5 (Washington, D. C.: American Psychiatric Association, 1973).
38. D. H. Barlow. Increasing Heterosexual Responsiveness in the Treatment of Sexual Deviation: A Review of the Clinical and Experimental Evidence, *Behavior Therapy* 4 (1973) 655-671.
39. L. Birk, W. Huddleston, E. Miller, and B. Cohler. Avoidance Conditioning for Homosexuality, *Archives of General Psychiatry* 25 (1971) 314-323.
40. Editorial. Behavior Therapy for Sex Problems, *Lancet* 1 (1973) 1295-1297.
41. J. Bancroft and I. Marks. Electric Aversion Therapy of Sexual Deviations, *Proceedings of the Royal Society of Medicine* 61 (1968) 796-799.

42. *Op. Cit.* Ref. 39.
43. S. Rachman and J. Teasdale. AVERSION THERAPY AND BEHAVIOUR DIS-ORDERS: AN ANALYSIS (London: Routledge & Kegan Paul, 1969).
44. M. Serber and J. Wolpe. "Behavior Therapy and Techniques," in SEXUAL BEHAVIORS: SOCIAL, CLINICAL, AND LEGAL ASPECTS, H. L. P. Resnik and M. E. Wolfgang, eds. (Boston: Little, Brown & Co., 1972) Chapter 11, pp 239-254.
45. *Op. Cit.* Ref. 30.
46. R. Hallam and S. Rachman. Theoretical Problems of Aversion Therapy, *Behavior Research and Therapy* 10 (1972) 341-353.
47. B. A. Tanner. Aversive Shock Issues: Physical Danger, Emotional Harm, Effectiveness and "Dehumanization." *Journal of Behavior Therapy and Experimental Psychiatry* 4 (1973) 113-115.
48. *Op. Cit.* Ref. 29.
49. *Op. Cit.* Ref. 39.
50. J. Bremer. ASEXUALIZATION (New York: Macmillan, 1959).
51. G. Sturup. "Castration: The Total Treatment," in SEXUAL BEHAVIORS: SOCIAL, CLINICAL, AND LEGAL ASPECTS, H. L. P. Resnik and M. E. Wolfgang, eds. (Boston: Little, Brown & Co., 1972) Chapter 18, pp 361–382.
52. *Op. Cit.* Ref. 22.
53. J. M. MacDonald, J. Money, S. Schaarer, J. R. Evrard, and R. Slovenko. Viewpoints: Castration for Rapists? *Medical Aspects of Human Sexuality* 732 (1973) 12-27.
54. Case Studies in Bioethics. Case 536. *Hastings Center Report* 5 (1975).
55. G. Dworkin. Can Convicts Consent to Castration? *Hastings Center Report* 5 (1975) 18-19.
56. J. Money. Use of an Androgen-Depleting Hormone in the Treatment of Male Sex Offenders, *The Journal of Sex Research* 6 (1970) 165-172.
57. J. Bancroft, G. Tennent, K. Loucas, and J. Kaas. The Control of Deviant Sexual Behavior by Drugs: 1. Behavioural Changes Following Oestrogens and Anti-Androgens, *British Journal of Psychiatry* 125 (1974) 310-315.
58. C. W. Dunn. Stilbestrol-Induced Gynecomastia in the Male, *Journal of the American Medical Association* 115 (1940) 2263-2264.
59. Personal communication. J. Money, M .D., Office of Psychohormonal Research, The Johns Hopkins Medical Institutions, June 24, 1975.
60. M. Goldstein. Brain Research and Violent Behavior, *Archives of Neurology* 30 (1974) 1-35.
61. F. Roeder, H. Orthner, and D. Muller. "The Stereotaxic Treatment of Pedophilic Homosexuality and Other Sexual Deviations," in

PSYCHOSURGERY, E. Hitchcock, L. Laitenen, and K. Vaernet, eds. (Springfield, Illinois: Charles C Thomas, 1972).

62. E. S. Valenstein. BRAIN CONTROL: A CRITICAL EXAMINATION OF BRAIN STIMULATION AND PSYCHOSURGERY (New York: John Wiley & Sons, 1973).

63. O. Andy. Neurosurgical Treatment of Abnormal Behavior, *American Journal of Medical Science* 132 (1966) 232-238.

64. W. H. Sweet. Treatment of Medically Intractable Mental Disease by Limited Frontal Leucotomy—Justifiable? *New England Journal of Medicine* 289 (1973) 1117-1125.

65. J. D. Hodson, Reflections Concerning Violence and the Brain, *Criminal Law Bulletin* 9 (1973) 684-702.

66. H. Baily, J. Dowling, and Y. E. Davies. The Control of Affective Illness by Cingulotractomy: A Review of 150 Cases, *Medical Journal of Australia* 2 (1973) 366-371.

67. J. Dietz. Hub Psychosurgery Draw $2 Million Suit, *Boston Globe* (1973) December 10.

68. Sol Rubin. "The Repeated or Multiple Offender," in LAW OF CRIMINAL CORRECTION (St. Paul, Minnesota: West Publishing Co., 2nd ed., 1973) Chapter 11, 470-478.

69. *Lessard v. Schmidt*, 349 F. Supp. 1078 (E.D. Wis. 1972); On appeal to the United States Supreme Court the judgment of the district court was vacated and the case remanded on procedural grounds. The district court then entered another order providing declaratory and injunctive relief, 379 F. Supp. 1376 (E. D. Wis. 1974). However, the Supreme Court again vacated the judgment and remanded for further consideration in light of another case, which held that the limitations of a federal court intervening in state proceedings apply to civil as well as criminal state proceedings, *Schmidt v. Lessard*, 95 S. Ct. 1943 (1975). A three-judge federal court then again reinstated its prior judgment. It held that state civil commitment procedures are not in "aid of nor closely related to any state interests underlying its criminal justice system, so as to be within the doctrine of federal non-intervention in pending state proceedings." However, the court noted that the *Lessard* case, which dealt with Wisconsin's civil commitment statutes, differed from the state's sex crimes law in that the purpose of the former was to treat individuals suffering from mental illness while the purpose of the latter was to protect society from the commission of further sex crimes, 413 F. Supp. 1318 (E.D. Wis. 1976).

70. *Commonwealth v. Page*, 159 N.E. 2d 82 (Mass. 1959).

71. *Baxstrom v. Herold*, 383 U.S. 107 (1966).

72. See, for example, *In re Ballay*, 482 F. 2d 648, 653-669 (D.C. Cir. 1973) (Proof beyond a reasonable doubt); *In re Hodges*, 325 Atl. 2d 605, 607 (D.C. App. 1974) (proof beyond a reasonable doubt); *Lessard v. Schmidt*, 349 F. Supp. 1078, 1095 (E.D. Wis. 1972) (proof beyond a reasonable doubt); *In re Pickles' Petition*, 170 So. 2d 603, 614 (Fla. Ct. App. 1954) (Proof beyond a reasonable doubt); *U.S. Ex Rel, Stachulak v. Coughlin*, 520 F. 2d 931 (Illinois 1975) where, under the Illinois Sexually Dangerous Persons Act, a person can be committed to the Director of Corrections for an indeterminate stay in lieu of a criminal prosecution, but the standard of proof must then be "beyond a reasonable doubt." Also see *People v. Pembrock*, 342 N.E. 2d 28 (Illinois 1976) in determining whether a person is such a sexually dangerous person, the standard is to be the same employed in determining criminal guilt (proof beyond a reasonable doubt). *Denton v. Commonwealth*, 383 S.W. 2d 681, 683 (Kentucky 1964) adopted proof beyond a reasonable doubt; *In re Levias*, 83 Wash. 2d 253, 254-256 (1973) where the standard was proof by clear, cogent, and convincing evidence; this was said by the court to be the civil counterpart of the criminal reasonable doubt standard. See, further, *Murel v. Baltimore City Criminal Court*, 407 U.S. 355, 359-365 (1972) (Douglas, J., dissenting) (proof beyond a reasonable doubt; majority did not reach the merits and *Andrews v. Commonwealth*, Mass. S. J. c1975—Mass.—(slip opinion) (proof beyond a reasonable doubt). California now requires the "beyond a reasonable doubt" standard of burden of proof. It also requires a unanimous jury verdict on the question of whether someone is a "mentally disordered sex offender." See *People v. Burnick*, 535 P. 2d 352 (1975) and *People v. Feagley*, 535 P. 2d 373 (1975). Surprisingly, these tightened standards have not substantially reduced the number of sex offenders judicially committed as sexual psychopaths to the Atascadero State Hospital (personal communication by Seymour Pollack, M.D., Chairman, Atascadero State Hospital Advisory Board).

73. *Commonwealth v. Lamb*, Mass. App. Ct. Adv. Sh. (1973 at 635-640).

74. *Commonwealth v. Andrews*, Mass. Adv. Sh. (1975).

75. *Commonwealth v. Bladsa*, Mass. Adv. Sh. 1675-1677 (1972).

76. *Commonwealth v. Dooley*, 232 A. 2d 45 (Pa. Super. 1967).

77. *Davy v. Sullivan*, 354 F. Supp. 1320 (M.D. Ala. 1973).

78. *Specht v. Patterson*, 386 U.S. 605, 608-609, 610 (1967).

79. *United States ex rel. Gerchman v. Maroney*, 355 F. 2d 302, 312 (3d Cir. 1966).

80. *In re Gault*, 387 US 1 (1967), 18.

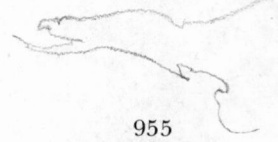

81. Under current California law (6300 California Welfare and Institutions Code, Amendment 1975), the court may commit a sex psychopath to a state hospital for an indeterminate period. (In California, sex psychopaths are referred to as mentally disabled sex offenders and, after conviction for a sexual offense, they may be deemed sexually dangerous to the health and safety of others by virtue of mental disease, disorder, or defect.) The statute also requires a determination of the mentally disordered sex offender's "amenability" to treatment within a state institutional setting. As of January 1, 1976, Assembly Bill 1229 allowed commitment of such persons, under specified judicial control, to private facilities and even to outpatient care, supervised by community mental health agencies.

82. *Huebner v. State, op. cit.*

83. *Jackson v. Indiana*, 406 US 715 (1972).

84. Notes and Comments. Civil Restraint, Mental Illness, and Right to Treatment, *Yale Law Journal* 77 (1967) 87-116.

85. *In re Maddox*, 351 Mich. 358 (1957).

86. *Miller v. Overholser*, 206 F. 2d 415 (D.C. Cir. 1953).

87. *People v. Feagley*, 535 P. 2d 373 (Calif. 1975).

88. *Millard v. Cameron*, 373 F. 2d 468 (1966).

89. G. H. Morris. THE MENTALLY ILL AND THE RIGHT TO TREATMENT (Springfield, Illinois: Charles C Thomas, 1970).

90. *Donaldson v. O'Connor*, 493 F. 2d 507 (1974). The Court of Appeals for the Fifth Circuit had affirmed the judgment of a jury verdict assessing both compensatory and punitive damages against the superintendent and another physician for intentionally and maliciously depriving patient Donaldson of his "constitutional right to liberty." It is interesting that for a period of 15 years Donaldson had unsuccessfully been seeking judicial relief. The United States Supreme Court upheld the finding that Dr. O'Connor had violated Donaldson's right to liberty by keeping him hospitalized as a nondangerous person, for 15 years without adequate treatment. See *O'Connor v. Donaldson*, 95 S. Ct. 2486 (1975); the case was remanded for a determination of the adequacy of the trial judge's instructions concerning the liability of the superintendent as a state official under the qualified immunity doctrine to determine whether he knew or should have known that the action of keeping Donaldson violated constitutional rights or whether he acted with malicious intent.

91. *Rouse v. Cameron*, 373 F. 2d 451 (D.D. Cir. 1966).

92. *Op. cit.*, Ref. 90.

Sex psychopath legislation

93. *Op. cit.*, Ref. 72.
94. *Nason v. Superintendent*, 353 Mass. 604, 233 N.E. 2d 908 (1968).
95. *Wyatt v. Stickney*, 325 F. Supp. 781 (Ala. 1971): 344 F. Supp. 373 (Ala. 1972): *Wyatt v. Aderholt*, 503 F. 2d 1305 (1974): *Wyatt v. Hardin*, —F. Supp.— (1975).
96. *Burnham v. Georgia*, 349 F. Supp. 1335 (N.D. Ga. 1972).
97. B. J. Ennis. PRISONERS OF PSYCHIATRY (New York: Harcourt, Brace, Jovanovich, 1972).
98. J. Hall. Psychiatry and Criminal Responsibility, *Yale Law Journal* 65 (1956) 761.
99. *Kaimowitz v. Michigan Department of Mental Health*, Civil No. 73-19434, Circuit Court Wayne County, Mich. (July 10, 1973).

ACKNOWLEDGMENTS TO CONTRIBUTORS

The program of the Group for the Advancement of Psychiatry, a nonprofit, tax-exempt organization, is made possible largely through the voluntary contributions and efforts of its members. For their financial assistance during the past fiscal year in helping it to fulfill its aims, GAP is grateful to the following:

Sponsors
Abbott Laboratories
Maurice Falk Medical Fund
Mrs. Carol Gold
Gralnick Foundation
The Grove School
The Holzheimer Fund
Ittleson Foundation, Inc.
Lederle Laboratories
Merck, Sharp & Dohme Laboratories
The Phillips Foundation
Roche Laboratories
Sandoz Pharmaceuticals
Schering-Plough Corporation
The Murray L. Silberstein Fund (Mrs. Alan H. Kalmus)
Smith, Kline & French Laboratories
Friends and Family of
    Bradley A. Stine MSSW, 1949-1976
Leo S. Weil Foundation

Donors
M. Aron Foundation
The Division Fund
McNeil Laboratories
Pfizer Pharmaceuticals, Inc.

OTHER RECENT PUBLICATIONS
GROUP FOR THE ADVANCEMENT OF PSYCHIATRY

No.	Title	Price
97	MYSTICISM: Spiritual Quest or Psychic Disorder?	$4.00
96	RECERTIFICATION: A Look at the Issues	2.50
95	THE EFFECT OF THE METHOD OF PAYMENT ON MENTAL HEALTH CARE PRACTICE	4.00
94	THE PSYCHIATRIST AND PUBLIC WELFARE AGENCIES	2.50
93	PHARMACOTHERAPY AND PSYCHOTHERAPY: Paradoxes, Problems and Progress	6.00
92	THE EDUCATED WOMAN: Prospects and Problems	4.00
91	THE COMMUNITY WORKER: A Response to Human Need	4.00

Orders amounting to less than $5.00 must be accompanied by remittance. All prices are subject to change without notice.

GAP publications may be ordered on a subscription basis. The current subscription cycle comprising the Volume IX Series covers the period from July 1, 1974 to June 30, 1977. For further information, write the Publications Office (see below).

Bound volumes of GAP publications issued since 1947 are also available which include GAP titles no longer in print and no longer available in any other form. A bound index of volumes (I through VII) has been published separately.

Please send your order and remittance to: Publications Office, Group for the Advancement of Psychiatry, 419 Park Avenue South, New York, New York 10016.

This publication was produced for the Group for the Advancement of Psychiatry by the Mental Health Materials Center, Inc., New York